Love and War:

A Southern Soldier's Struggle Between Love and Duty

Dr. Robert H. Crewdson

MARINER
PUBLISHING

BUENA VISTA, VIRGINIA

Copyright © 2009 by Robert H. Crewdson
Map Copyright © by Rick Britton

1 3 5 7 9 10 8 6 4 2

Library of Congress Control Number: 2001012345
Love and War:
A Southern Soldier's Struggle Between Love and Duty

Author
Includes Bibliographical References

p. cm.

1. Thurman, Merit Branch, 1825–1864   2. Humphrey, Jane Rosser,
1844–1886 3. Confederate States of America, Army of Northern Virginia,
Company C, 14th Virginia Regiment, Armistead's Brigade, Pickett's Division 4.
Soldiers—Virginia, Biography 5. Fluvanna County, Virginia—biography

I. Crewdson, Robert Henry, 1933— II. Title.

ISBN 13: 978-0-9820172-4-1 (softcover : alk. paper)

ISBN 10: 0-9820172-4-3

Mariner Publishing
A division of
Mariner Media, Inc.
131 West 21st Street
Buena Vista, VA 24416
Tel: 540-264-0021
http://www.marinermedia.com

Printed in the United States of America

This book is printed on acid-free paper meeting the
requirements of the American Standard for Permanence of
Paper for Printed Library Materials.

The Compass Rose and Pen are trademarks of Mariner Media, Inc.

Dedication

This book is dedicated to the courageous Southern women who did the best they could do for their husbands, their homes, farms and families while their husbands were fighting the invading Union Army. These women suffered all kinds of deprivation, especially when the Union Army had control of the area in which they lived. The Southern women, like Jane, are the unsung heroes of the South.

Contents

Introduction

In the late 1950s, while training to be a hospital corpsman at a naval center in Maryland, I visited my Aunt Ethel Moran in nearby Ridley Park, Pennsylvania. She showed me a box of letters written by a relative of ours to his wife during the "War Between the States." They were written by a Southern soldier named Meredith "Merit" Branch Thurman to his sweetheart, Jane Rosser Humphrey, who married him during the war. At the time I was incredibly busy with my studies and was looking forward to my own engagement and marriage. I was also taking a University of Alabama correspondence course on St. Paul's travels, in the event I decided to study for the Episcopal ministry after service in the navy. I was not interested in reading Merit's letters, so I asked Aunt Ethel if she would jot down for me their main points. These I still have.

Twenty-five years later, when I was in my middle forties, I started getting interested in my family genealogy. I remembered the letters Aunt Ethel had shared with me and tried to locate them. She had returned them to her aunt—to whom they belonged—however, and because of the passage of time many family members had died, so it was not an easy task.

Eventually I tracked down a cousin who ran a bar in West Grove, Pennsylvania, who told me to write her cousin, Katherine Shortlidge, in Missouri. When I contacted Katherine she wrote back saying that she indeed had the precious box of letters. I asked her if she would photocopy them and send the copies to me which she most graciously did. I first began to transcribe Merit's letters by writing them out in my own handwriting. Whenever I could not decipher a word, I would photocopy the page, underline the troublesome word, and ask Katherine if she could figure it out from the original letter. Usually she could, but there were several times when she could not. I am very indebted to Katherine Shortlidge for all the work she did in helping me get as close to Merit's original words as possible.

After I had finished this process, I sent copies of Merit's letters—in my own printing—to a cousin in Philadelphia who had also become interested in our family genealogy and asked him to type them. He had a secretary who had no work for a week while he was away, so he asked her to type the letters as a "special project." It was not an easy job as I had printed out the letters exactly as they had been written with few capitals or paragraph breaks, little punctuation, and lots of misspelled words. When my cousin returned from his trip and asked his secretary how she did on the letters, she said they were so precious and then broke down in tears.

When I re-typed the letters for this book, I used both the zeroxed original copies from my cousin and my hand-printed translations to avoid any mistakes the typist may have made as they are very difficult to reproduce in the format in which they were originally written. Merit spelled words as they sounded and really did quite well for someone living in that era who had little education. He always capitalized the letter "R," for example, and oftentimes the letter "S." Most of the time, Merit also left out the letter "e" when it is silent such as in "som," "hav," and "liv." Only a few times did he use an apostrophe, thus "wouldn't" became "wouldent" and "shouldn't" was written "shouldent." He spelled "care" as "kear" and "sincere" as "sencear." Those were his main mistakes. His sweetheart Jane, however, had evidently learned how to write. Maybe her mother—who signed her name with an "X"—insisted that she learn. To help the reader, I have left three blank spaces between Merit's sentences because he left no gaps at all. I have also put the address and complimentary close of each letter on the left side of the letters, as they tended to be all over the top and bottom of each letter.

An important issue that I had to face in the beginning was Meredith's name. His brothers called him "Merit," his marriage certificate lists it as "Merritt," while his service records show it as "Meredith." I had to make a choice, so I chose "Merit" assuming that it was his family nickname. Since "Meredith" could be a male or female's name, he may have preferred not to use it. Also, "Merit" is much easier to say than "Meredith." Merit called his wife Jane Rosser Humphrey by her middle name, "Rosser." In my work on the letters, I have used "Merit" and "Jane" rather than "Meredith" and "Rosser."

Shortly after this whole process was completed, my son, Robert, was starting his college application process. We discovered that the Daughters of the Confederacy in Manassas, Virginia—near where we lived in Haymarket—provided scholarships for high school students who could prove that they were related to Confederate soldiers. Robert applied for the scholarship but it was given instead to a young lady. This scholarship process, of course, made us prove our relationship to Private Merit Branch Thurman. He was one of my great-great grandfathers on my mother's side of our family. Unfortunately, since Merit evidently did not preserve Jane's letters, we only get one side of their poignant correspondence. From Merit's letters, however, we can oftentimes determine what Jane must have said in her missives. The collection of letters also includes several to Jane from Merit's brother, Robert. These give us some insight into the closeness of their family. The letters herein reproduced are indeed as precious as my cousin's secretary described them. Merit, as the reader will soon discover, had divided loyalties between Jane—who became his wife on December 2, 1862—and the Southern Army.

Sometimes Merit included poems in his letters to Jane. They beautifully illustrate his inner conflict between love and war. One letter written from Culpeper County on June 12, 1863—addressed to "My dear loving wife"—includes the following at the end:

> the happyest times I ever spent in all my life
> was when I was with my dear good little loving wife
> the happyest hours I ever se
> was when I had you along with me
> our time is short our days are few
> the happyest hours I ever spent was along with you
> the good days we hav spent is past and gone
> and now the hard times is coming on ...

Another poem written by Merit to Jane appears at the bottom of a letter written from a camp near Richmond on April 11, 1864, addressed to "MrS Jane R Thurman." It reads:

When thiS you Se remember me
though many miles apart we be
our days on earth are few
the happyest times I ever spent was along with you
the happyest hours I ever spent in all my life
was when I was along with my little wife

He missed her so much and feared for her safety. As with many of the Southern soldiers, he went AWOL—"absent without leave"—when his regiment was near her home in Fluvanna County, Virginia. Thus the title of this book—*Love and War: A Southern Soldier's Struggle Between Love and Duty.*

Chapter 1:
A Boatman Meets a Girl

Merit Branch Thurman was born on April 29, 1825. His parents were Hezekiah Bowls Thurman and Nancy Ann McGruder. Born in 1797, Nancy was the daughter of Zepheniah McGruder and Frances Sublett. Hezekiah, whose parents are unknown, was born in 1790 in Chesterfield, Virginia. Hezekiah and Nancy were married in Chesterfield on April 14, 1813, and Merit Branch Thurman—their sixth child—was born in that locality.

Little is known of Merit's childhood or young adulthood. From his Civil War letter of December 24, 1862, however, we know that he had been working in the Chesterfield coal mines sometime around 1852. In the letter Merit noted that a Yankee deserter, who had joined the infantry company of which his brothers Robert and Grandison were members, was an old acquaintance he had worked with at the coal mines ten years earlier. Since the men of the unit—Company D, 41st Virginia Infantry Regiment—were recruited primarily from the Clover Hill Mines, it makes sense that a Northern man who had worked in these mines would desert to Company D to be reunited with all of his former workmates.[1]

As a whole the Clover Hill Mines were known by name of the nearby town—Midlothian. These coal mines were a major coal source in the entire South, raising the valuable resource on a large scale from deep in the pits.[2] This was very dangerous work as explosions frequently rocked the caverns.[3] The mines were connected to the James River—where there was river and canal transportation—via a short thirteen-mile railway.[4]

Merit became a boatman on the nearby James River and Kanawha Canal sometime after 1852, a fact that makes one wonder whether, as a mine employee, he had been involved in coal transportation. The decade of the 1850s was the James River and Kanawha Canal's most prosperous time.[5] Boatmen must have been in demand. During the 1850s there were also several connecting canals that ran up tributaries of the James River. One of these was the four-and-one-half-mile-long "Rivanna Connection" along the lower portion of the Rivanna River, which flows diagonally through Fluvanna County. The Rivanna River Company ran this canal. From Merit's letter of December 6, 1860, we know that he worked on the Rivanna River and certainly the James River as well. The boatmen brought goods up the river from Richmond (in flat-bottomed bateau-boats), and took tobacco, flour, and other products back to Richmond and often all the way to the Tidewater for shipment overseas. It seems that the flour grown in Virginia—and milled at the various mills along the rivers and canals—resisted mold when shipped to South America. The production of this commodity, therefore, brought prosperity to the mills along the rivers where the boats operated.

The boatmen also operated packet, or passenger, boats on the rivers and canals. The arrival of a packet boat at a boat landing was a major social event for a riverside community. It was then that the local folks would gather to visit, see and be seen, and catch up on the news of the day.[6] One such Rivanna River town was Union Mills in Fluvanna County. During the 1850s Union Mills was growing into a prosperous industrial center (which would thrive until about 1900).[7] Union Mills contained a merchant mill, a grist mill, and a cotton factory called the Virginia Union Company.[8] The factory employed 100 people and operated 1,500 cotton spindles and twelve power looms.[9] A merchant mill is one which is commercial, which takes in the wheat and grinds and sells it and ships it as flour.[10] The town featured comfortable houses for the accommodation of eighteen or twenty factory families, a tan yard, and a Methodist house of worship, not to mention the proprietors' elegant dwellings.[11]

The family of Merit's future wife, Jane, lived at or near Union Mills. Her father was a miller at Union Mills (and Merit and Jane were later married at the Methodist Church there). Only a teenager at the time, young Jane Rosser Humphrey must have caught Merit's eye while his bateau was stopped at Union Mills. This is the best explanation as to how a boatman from Chesterfield County met a woman from Union Mills in Fluvanna County. Soon thereafter, Merit wrote Jane from Buck Island just north over the Fluvanna County line in Albemarle County. This was a little further upriver than large mule-drawn ninety-three-foot-long by fourteen-foot-wide freighters could go.[12] Thus, Merit must have been operating the smaller sixty-foot-long by up to seven-foot-wide bateau boats which were poled by the boatmen.[13] According to Newton Bond Jones, there was a mill located near Buck Island.[14] Merit's letter from Buck Island is as follows:

December The 6th . 1860

Miss Jane Ross. I embrace the
present opotunity of writing a few
Lines to you to inform you that I have
not forgotten you. yet I will be up about
The tenth of the month. My ink is bad
My pen is keen I love you better then
all the girls I have ever seen I Rather Se you
then any one in the world I of you evry hour
in the day. nothing more at present.
Yours cencearly M. B. Thurman
Your affectionate friend
Buck Island
Albemarle County
VA

Evidently, for Merit's relationship with Jane to blossom, either her mother asked for a reference as to his character or he voluntarily provided one. From what he wrote, Mr. A. W. Trabue must have been either a neighbor or close friend of Merit's family.

Chesterfield January 15 1861

This is to certify that I have known Mr. M
Thurman from his childhood to this time and
He has always been an Industrious and a honest man
and never known him to be a married man or ever
heard of any such a thing and I take pleasure in
saying his parrants stands fair and respectable

Very Respectible Your
A W Trabue

There appear to be initials under A. W. Trabue's name—possibly "J. P."—which may stand for "Justice of the Peace", or the person who wrote the letter for Mr. Trabue.

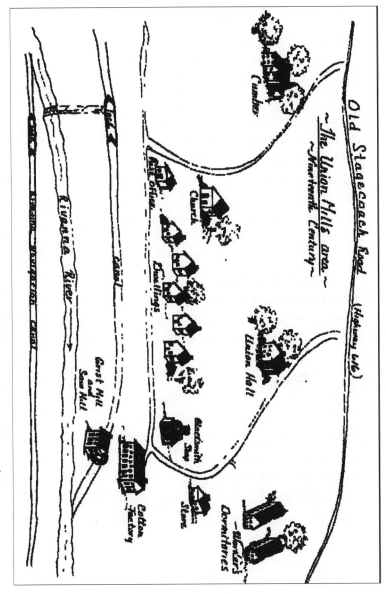

Hand drawn map of Union Mills provided by The Fluvanna County Historical Society

Chapter 1 Endnotes

~

1   William D. Henderson, *41st Virginia Infantry* (Lynchburg, 1986), p. 4.
2   Bettie Woodson Weaver, "The Mines of Midlothian," *Virginia Cavalcade* 11, no. 3:40–47, p. 40.
3   Ibid., p. 44.
4   Ibid., p. 43.
5   Kent Druyvesteyn, "With Great Vision: The James River and Kanawha Canal," *Virginia Cavalcade* 21, no. 3:22–47, p. 28.
6   Ellen Miyagawa, "The James River and Kanawha Canal in Fluvanna," *The Bulletin of the Fluvanna Historical Society*, no.33:1–35, p.26.
7   W. E. Trout III and Peter C. Runge, *The Rivanna Scenic River Atlas* (Lexington, Virginia, 1992).
8   Minnie Lee McGehee, "Old Mills of Fluvanna," *The Bulletin of the Fluvanna Historical Society*, No. 10 & 11. October, 1970, p. 27.
9   Ibid., p. 27.
10   Minnie Lee McGehee, *Communication*, January 30, 2009.
11   Minnie Lee McGehee, "Old Mills of Fluvanna," *The Bulletin of the Fluvanna Historical Society*, No. 10 & 11. October, 1970, p. 27.
12   Minnie Lee McGehee and W. E. Trout III, *Mr. Jefferson's River: The Rivanna* (Charlottesville, 2001), p. 39–40.
13   Ibid., p.13.
14   Newton Bond Jones, "Charlottesville and Albemarle County, Virginia, 1819–1860," (U.Va. Dissertation, 1950), p. 101.

Chapter 2:

A Boatman Enlists in the Confederate Army

*

There exists no correspondence from Merit to Jane from December 1860 until June 14, 1861. There are several possibilities as to why. Jane's mother may have cooled off their seeing each other until Jane was a little older. Merit's boat may have been making regular trips up and down the Rivanna and he did not have the time to write. Also, Merit may have simply lost interest for a while. (Additionally, the letters may have been distributed among members of my family and then lost. These are all speculations.) However, Merit did see Jane in the spring of 1861 and he definitely wrote her as the following letter of June 14, 1861, testifies.

Merit had evidently promised Jane that he would not volunteer for the Southern Army. When he thought he would be drafted, however, he went ahead and volunteered so that he could be with some of his friends (and possibly his brothers). Merit could not have been drafted that early in the war. Confederate conscription began in April 1862.[1] At Palmyra, in Fluvanna

County—according to his military record—Merit on May 10, 1861, enlisted for one year in the Fluvanna Rifle Guard. This volunteer company was transported to Richmond by boat, first on the Rivanna River Canal, and then on the James River and Kanawha Canal.[2] On May 12, 1861, at the capital of the Confederacy, the Fluvanna Rifle Guard was mustered into state service and drilled by the Virginia Military Institute cadets.[3] The Fluvanna Rifle Guard was also known as Company C of the 14th Virginia Regiment and its captain was Robert H. Poore, a lawyer from Palmyra.[4] Virginia governor John Letcher assigned James Gregory Hodges, a prominent physician from Portsmouth, as the colonel of the 14th Virginia Infantry. David Godwin, an attorney, became the unit's lieutenant colonel, while physician William White was made its major.[5] At the end of May, the 14th Virginia was sent to Jamestown, Virginia—on the peninsula between the York and the James Rivers—to garrison and complete construction of Fort Allen. John Bankhead Magruder, a former U.S. Army officer, was soon thereafter assigned to the Department of the Peninsula. His mission was to oversee the defensive line from Hampton to Yorktown and to defend workers constructing a fort at Jamestown Island.[6] Merit explained to Jane in the following letter that it was "out of his power" to come to see her. The local post office was overwhelmed with mail and the mail was slow.[7]

[excuse me for writing with pencil I could not get any ink]
James Town
June the 14th 1861

miss Rosser my dear friend. I take my pen in hand this
evening to write a few lines to you to inform you that I
am living yet and well and hearty and I hope when you

receive these few lines that it may find you injoying the same
blessings. I would be happy to se you at this time but it
is out of my power to com up now I have bin expecting a
letter from you. you promust me when I wrote to you that
you would write to me again I wrote to you when I was in
richmond but I have never received any answer when I
wrote to you I dident expect to leave richmond as soon as I
did I rite severel letters for sum of the other men that was
with me in richmond and letters was directed to Richmond
to them and was sent on down to jamestown and I expected
that if you wrote to me that your letter would bin sent on
down too. but I have not Received an answer from you I
hope you havent taken any offence with me if I have ever
hert your feelings I am sorry for it you have never hert
anyone and you have treated me well and kind and who
all of the family is treated me the same. I promust you
that I wouldent join the volunteers but I found it was best
rather than to be drafted I never intend to act a coward a
great many of my acquantances was going at the time and
I thought I would go on with them that I was acquainted
with so is I would be better satisfied travling about threw
strange parts of the world sum of my old acquaintances
is hear with me that was raised with me I expected to get
with two of my brothers but they belong to another company
at the time I joined I could not get off please don't think
hard of me I will try and com back to se you in the fall if
I live to se that time it will be a joyfull time with me. I
intends to fullfill evry promas that I hav ever made if I ever
liv to get back I will never forsaken you this side of my
grave and I hope that you will never forsaken me I want
you to write to me if you pleas you need not write no great
long letter without you chose the is an one request that I ask

of you and that is from my heart and it is the last request
that I will ask of you. I want you to wate for me untell I
com back and I want you to write me word that you will
weight for me and that will be a great consolation to me   I
would not ask that request of you that I am bound hear
now and I cant se you and I dident arrange things with you
is I intended before I left   if you don't grant the faver that
I ask you the will be no more pleasure for me   if you will
say that you will weight for me the is nothing will stop me
from coming back except death   I will start back if I liv   if
I die on the way the is sum people about there is tirble to tel
you lies or anything to put you against me but what ever I
tel you you may rely upon it   I never intend to vary from
my word   they can say anything they chose now I am not
there to protect myself. what I say to you is sincear and
truth from my heart and yet I hope the time will come that
we will meat to never part   I may not have long to live   I
may not have long hear to tarry but I can say that you are
the only girl that ever I loved well enough . . . [Sentence
not clear] . . . and I can say that you are the only girl that
I ever saw that sooted my mind. if I never se you anymore
I hope that you may do well and I hope when we both . . .
[Remainder of letter not available]

While at Fort Allen, Merit's regiment not only endured bad food, limited supplies, crowded living conditions, and hard, dirty, and boring work, it also suffered from widespread disease because of the era's limited knowledge of field sanitation.[8] The 14th Virginia stayed at Fort Allen until August 2 when it was moved to Land's End (or Mrs. Curtis's farm).[9] On August 7 the 14th Virginia was a part of a 5,000-man force that attempted to lure the Federals away from Fort Monroe for a battle, but this attempt failed.[10] While in Hampton, General Magruder ordered the town burned so that the Federals or blacks could not use the houses for winter quarters.[11]

After the action at Hampton the 14th Virginia marched to Mulberry Island Point which it reached on August 17 and stayed a few days before returning to Mrs. Curtis's farm at Land's End.[12] Upon arrival, Merit wrote Jane the following letter:

August 17th 1861

My dear frend
I have the pleasure of writing to you onest more to let you kno that I have not forgotten yet   I Received your kind letter at warrick court house a few days ago and was glad to hear from you but had much rather se you   I want to see you badly   I hope it will not be long now but I don't kno yet   I hav bin threw som Ruff times since I rote to you last but I am not hirt yet   We had a battle at hampton elizabeth county on the 7th of august about one oclock in the night we killed 18 yankeys   the was not one of our men hirt   we Run them off then burnt the town up   we are now 20 mile this side of hamton at mulberry island but I don't kno how long we will stay hear   it is not worth while for you to write to me now   I don't know where will go from hear   I will write to you again when I stop long enough at a place   I write this to let you kno I hav not forgotten you nor I never will forget you the longest day I liv   I lov you so well I cant forget you I never se no girl that I lov is well and I no I never will again   you wrote to me to write you word when I was coming but I cant tell you yet   I wish it was so I could com now but I cant   there is nothing but death will stop me

from coming when I get off from hear   you must Remember
me and I will Remember you   I lov you better then all the
world and if I thought I never would se you any more I
would Ruined   I know [can't make out word] to write more
I cant explain all to you now   giv my love to all the family
Yours sencearly
M. B. Thurman
your loving frend until death

The outside of the letter reads: "I have a great deal of
news to tell you when I se you ˙ I cant write all to you that I want
to write   I will write to you another time."

On October 14, the regiment was assigned to Col.
Thomas P. August's brigade.[13] Merit had evidently received
a letter via a Mr. Wescoat, who probably brought packages
and possibly the news from home to the various soldiers from
Fluvanna County. As usual, there were problems with the mail,
so Merit wrote at the end of the following letter to Jane to "direct
your letter to james town Island 14 Regiment Virginia in kear
of capt R H poore." (Why he asked Jane to send her letter to
Jamestown is not known unless it was the nearest post office or
he expected to be there for a few days with his company.) Merit
sent the following letter from Lands End, where Company C
would stay through December:

Lands end
October the 26th 1861

Miss Rosser my dear friend I take my pen in hand this
morning to write to you to let you know that I hav not
forgotten you you must excuse me for not writing sooner   I

received your kind affectionate letter the sixth of October
and I was glad to hear from you   I would be glad to se you
and talk with you   I had rather se you than any boddy in
the world but it is so that I cant se you now at this time but
I hope the time will not be long in I hope you will not think
hard of me not coming up to se you   I would com if I could
I am bound hear for a while but I will be free again in six
months from now   then I will com if I live   you may depend
on me to do all that I promised you and I will depend on
you to do as you said   I love you and don't love know one
else and I never intend to forsake you unless you first forsake
me   that is all that I can say   you said in your letter that
you hope that I would not think none the less of you for
expressing your self so plain to me but I think the more of
you for it.   I hope that you will not think none the less of me
for expressing my self so plain to you   I cant se you to talk to
you so I must write   excuse me for my short letter   I received
the present that you sent me by mr wescoat whitch I was
much oblige to you   I will give you more than that if I liv
to se you again   I havent time to write much now   I want
to write you a good letter the next time   you must write to
me as soon as you can   the is nothing affords me is much
pleasure is to Receive a letter from you   I have no news of
importance to write to you this time whitch I don't expect
would be news to you   giv my love to all your folks   make
your self contented and do the best you can   when I com
back again I will be your frend   I lov you better then all the
world   it is know secret   I don't kear who knows it   fare well
for a while   I may never se you again but as long is I liv I
will liv in hopes   write as soon is you can   don't fail
yours sincearly
M. B. Thurman

your affectionate frend
untell death
direct your letter to james town Island
14 Regiment Virginia in kear of
Capt R H poore

Merit penned another letter from Land's End in Warwick County saying that he did not have much hope in attending the marriage of Jane's older sister. Merit had also heard from Nat—N. B. Bacon—who was married to Jane's sister, Ellen.

Lands end warrick county Va
November the 30th 1861

my dear Rosser   I take my pen in hand to write a few more
lines to you to let you know that I am well at this time and
hope when you Receive this it may find you injoying the
same blessings   I Received your kind letter which was a
great pleasure to me   you must excuse me for not writing
to you before now   we hav bin about ten mile from this
place   we hav bin back about seven or eight days   I hav
bin so buissy that I dident hav time to write   I hav written
so much to you that I hardly know what to write   I think
of you night and day   I cant think any more of you then I
do   you wrote me word that miss caroline was going to be
married and I must com and se her married   I thank her for
the invertation but I don't expect I can com is soon is that
I may com up in january but I don't know yet   I want to
se you badly but I cant se you now but I hope the time will
soon Role around that I will be there withe you   I havent
much to write now   I had Rather se you and talk to you if
I could   I dream about you som times three or four nights

in succesion I dream som mighty good dreams about you   I
havent any more of importance to write this time   I will
com up as soon is I can   You must write as soon as you can
I think more of you then evry boddy in the world   I herd
from nat a few days ago   I will write to him in a few days
nothing more but Remains your affectionate frend   give my
love to all the family and all inquireing frends
M B Thurman
direct your letter to james Town
Island   14th Regmt va volentears
In kear of capt R H poor

Chapter 2 Endnotes

1   James I. Robertson Jr., Professor of History, VPI & SU, *Communication*, November 19, 2008.

2   Edward R. Crews and Timothy A. Parrish, *14th Virginia Infantry* (Lynchburg, 1995), p. 5.

3   Ibid., p. 7.

4   Ibid., p. 4.

5   Ibid., p. 7.

6   Ibid., p. 9–10.

7   Ibid., p. 8.

8   Ibid., p. 11.

9   Janet B. Hewitt, ed., *Supplement to the Official Records* (Wilmington, NC, 1998), p. 368.

10   Ibid., p. 12.

11   Ibid.

12   Ibid., p. 368.

13   Crews and Parrish, loc. cit., p.14

Chapter 3:
A Soldier Takes a Wife

Merit's first letter of 1862 was dated February 16. At the time the 14th Virginia was still in its Warwick County winter encampment at Mulberry Island on Minor's Creek. It had rained a lot and food continued to be a problem.[1] The only bright spot in life at Mulberry Island that winter was General Magruder's decision to allow seven-day furloughs for home visits.[2] Unfortunately, there was no way Merit could travel to Union Mills and back in that time period unless part of the trip was by train. He was hoping to try, however. A Mr. Whitehurst had visited the regiment, delivering things to the men from Fluvanna County which included two pairs of socks for Merit from his Union Mills sweetheart. Socks were often in short supply and were especially needed in winter when the men often wore two pairs simultaneously to keep their feet warm.

Mulberry Island   warrick county Va
February the 16th 1862

Miss Rosser   I embrace the opotunity of writing a few

lines to you to let you know that I am well at this time and hope when these few lines coms to hand it may find you injoying the same blessings I Received your letter a few days ago and I Received two pare of socks by Mr. Whitehurst which I was verry thankfull to you for them I will not forget you for your kindness to me I expects to be up the tenth of march I will be sure to com if I can if I don't com then I will com soon after if the is any possuble chance to get off I will be certain to com The is som talk of sending our Regiment to norfolk but I hope it will not be so I hav no good news of importance to write to you Times is getting hard in som parts from the account the papers gives but times be good or bad I intends to fullfull all promises that I have made to you when I get there the is nothing can brake the love and Respect I have for you except it is death I would be glad to se you if I could The is nothing would afford is much pleasure I havent any more of importance to write this time I would like to write som particulars to you but I don't Reccon it will be long now before I will se you giv my love and Respects to all your folks nothing more but Remains your tru frend
Yours sencearly
M. B.Thurman to miss Jane R Humphrey

Rite as soon is you can if I don't com
14th Regmt James Town Island
in kear of cap't R H poore

On February 7–8, 1862, Union Gen. Ambrose E. Burnside landed a division of Federal troops on Roanoke Island, North Carolina, and captured it along with its 2,500 Confederate defenders.[3] Union forces were now threatening the North Carolina coast as well as southeastern Virginia. On March 7 the 14th Virginia packed up its Tidewater encampment and marched to Kings Mill Wharf, about fifteen miles west of Mulberry Island, where it was jammed aboard a steamer bound for City Point, Virginia, (at the confluence of the James and Appomattox Rivers).[4] The following day the men of the 14th Virginia climbed onto trains at City Point. They chugged into Suffolk, Virginia, that evening.[5] There they remained until April 2 when they were marched off to North Carolina. They did not return to Suffolk until early May.[6] The 14th Virginia Infantry did not see combat in North Carolina; it only served to keep the Federals in check.[7] The men had been on active duty for roughly a year now and had done little beyond drill, dig, guard, watch, and fight homesickness, disease, and boredom.[8] Merit's one-year enlistment would be up on May 10, and, as he wrote to Jane, he planned to come home then.

There were also several administrative changes for the regiment in early 1862. From January to April, the 14th Virginia was part of Brig. Gen. Lafayette McLaw's Division. Afterwards it was transferred to Brig. Gen. Lewis A. Armistead's Brigade of Brig. Gen. Benjamin Huger's Division.[9]

In the following letter Merit mentioned Ben Pace, Jim Harlow, and Walker Tyler as men who visited him in camp when they came down "from home." All three were members of Company H of the 57th Virginia Infantry, Armistead's Brigade, and from the reference it appears that they had been home on leave. Merit also mentioned that he received a letter from Nat Bacon from "Southham"—probably Southampton—and that he did not get to visit with him. Nat was a private in the 57th Virginia which had already left for North Carolina. Nat's record is as follows: "Bacon, Nathaniel D. Machinist, enlisted 7/22/61 at Charlottesville in Company H. Present through 6/62. Deserted 6/27/62; rejoined company 3/11/63, Captured 10/11/64 at Front Royal. To Point Lookout, MD. Took oath and released 5/12/65. Residence: Fluvanna County."[10]

Suffolk   nancemond county
March 30th   1862

dear miss Rosser   I embrace the opotunity of writing to you to let you know that I hav not forgotten you yet   I am very sorry that I failed to com up is I wrote you word that was coming the first of march. I would of com but I could not get off so you must excuse me for not coming   you may look for me the tenth of may   I will be certain to be ther then without fail if nothing happens   I am now at Suffolk nancemond county   our Regement is ordered to north carolina   we expects to start in a day or two   we will go by railroad   it is about one hundred and 25 mile from where we is now   the fifty seventh Regemt is bin hear and left a few days before I got hear   I Received a letter from nat a few days ago from southam didnt get with him   we are going on the same cours that he is gone when we start from here   ben pace and jim harlow and walker tyler com down hear to se us when they com down from home   You must write to me as soon is you can   I want to hear from you badly   I had much rather se you but I know the time will not be long now   I love you is well now is ever did if not better   I would Run away and com up to se you but the laws is verry strict now they will not admit anyone to ride on the cares now without a written permit from his captain and Signed by the kirnal I beleave evry town in virginia under marshal laws   when

you write direct your letter to suffolk nancemond county Va
and I will be certain to get it whether I am hear or not the
letter is sent on to the 14th Regmt give my best love and
Respects to your mother and all the famly nothing more
but remaining your frend untell death.
Yours sencearly
M B Thurman
Suffolk nancemond county Va

We now come to a four-month gap in Merit's letters to Jane. Whether some of the letters were lost or our Confederate protagonist was simply too busy to write is not known. Also, Merit was confined to a hospital for a while during this period and that possibly made it difficult for him to write. A lot happened to the 14th Virginia Infantry during these four months. Merit and the 14th Virginia were back in Suffolk in early May but departed on May 12 for Petersburg where they arrived on the sixteenth. Thirteen days later, on May 29, they took a train to Richmond.[11] On April 4, 1862, Union Gen. George B. McClellan—along with an army of over 100,000 men—began his march up the Peninsula toward Richmond, arriving near the capital on May 24.[12] General Huger's Division, of which the 14th Virginia was a part, did not get into the first day's fight at the Battle of Seven Pines on May 31. On the second day of the action, however, the 14th Virginia participated in the Confederate attack and was repulsed taking forty-seven casualties.[13] The 14th Virginia Infantry then remained on picket duty until June 29.

On June 28 a regimental roster showed that the 14th Virginia had 449 men present and 261 absent, with many of them sick with dysentery, chronic diarrhea, malaria, and

33

typhoid.[14] According to his military record, that same day Merit was taken to a hospital and evidently missed the absolute slaughter at the Battle of Malvern Hill on July 1. As part of the Confederate right flank, General Armistead's three regiments—including the 14th Virginia and several that were attached—assaulted an amazingly strong Federal position on Malvern Hill and failed, taking 388 casualties.[15] For its effort the 14th Virginia lost seventy-five men, including twenty-four killed or mortally wounded.[16] That afternoon the regiment's battle flag was shot through forty-seven times. The large number of casualties told the story. Confederate forces lost 5,355 at Malvern Hill—Union losses totaled 3,214.[17]

It is not known when Merit was released from the hospital, but he evidently received some leave time as his August 1 letter mentioned a visit to his mother. He also noted that it was too hot for him to visit Jane plus he lacked a pass necessary to float up the James River on a packet boat. Merit wrote that he was getting tired of "Souldiering" and that "they are trying to keep all in the servis they can."

Until mid August of 1862, the 14th Virginia watched General McClellan's Army of the Potomac at Harrison's Landing on the James River from upriver at Drewry's Bluff.[18] During July, General Huger, because of his poor showing during the Seven Days' Battles around Richmond, was replaced as division commander by Maj. Gen. Richard H. Anderson.

Steven Gardner—who Merit mentioned in the subsequent letter—must have married Jane's sister, Elizabeth. (In 1855 William Page had married another of Jane's sisters, Irene, at Union Mills. Later, on December 2, 1862, Page would be a witness at Merit and Jane's wedding.) By the time the following was written, Nat Bacon had deserted and was back in Fluvanna County. Merit penned a note to him that was not preserved.

Chesterfield
August   the   1.   1862

Miss Rosser my dear friend   I with great pleasure seat my Self this morning to write to you to let you know that I am well at the present time and I hope when you receive these few lines it may find you injoying the same blessings   I received your kind interresting letter which I was truly glad to hear from you but I had much rather se you   I am now in camp near drewy Bluffs   I would of com up to se you when I was at my mothers but the wether was so warm and disagreable that I could not walk up there and had no pasport to ride on the packet so I concluded that I would go back to camp and com up Sum other time   I will try and get a ferlow before long and com up sum other time   I will try and get a ferlow before long and com and if I cant get a ferlow I will com any how   I am sorry that I failed to fullfill the promises that I maid you but must excuse me   I could not do any better   you may look for me in about four or five weeks from now   I am getting tired of Souldiering   I will try and get of all together if I can but though they are trying to keep all in servis they can   I nothing more of importance to write this time   The is know fighting going on hear   none at the present time but we don't know what time we will get in to a fight   we can hear the canan firing verry rapidly down below us   I supposes it down below city point   give my best love and respect to mr page and his family   I forgot to mention I would be glad to be up then and se old Steven

Gardener and miss betty married it is right funny I
dident think she would hav him old steven I must improve
Som nothing more. I Remains your affectionate frend and
forever will Remain So
Yours Sincearly
M. B. Thurman to miss J. R. H.
direct your letter to Richmond to the 14th Va Regmt
In kear Capt He poore and will get it
I write a few lines to nat

pleas send it to him

Union forces in Virginia were now divided and
ineffective. General McClellan's Army of the Potomac was
sitting idle on the James River below Richmond while Maj.
Gen. John Pope's Army of Virginia was just getting up a head
of steam in the northern part of the state. If these two Federal
hosts were combined, however, they would be far too strong for
Confederate Gen. Robert E. Lee's Army of Northern Virginia
to handle. On July 13, therefore, Lee dispatched 24,000 men
northward under Gen. "Stonewall" Jackson, who clashed with
two Union divisions at Cedar Mountain on August 9.[19] On
August 13, Lee—knowing that McClellan's army was being
withdrawn by river transport to reinforce Pope—started the
balance of his army north under Maj. Gen. James Longstreet.
Anderson's Division followed by train to Louisa Court House
on August 16. Ever attempting to maintain the initiative, Lee
planned to attack Pope before McClellan could get to him with
his army.[20]

Lee—with his 55,000-man army finally assembled—soon
faced Pope along the Rappahannock River. Lee then took a

calculated gamble and sent Jackson around Pope's army, going first west to Salem and then east to Manassas Junction where he captured Pope's supply depot and cut the railroad. "Stonewall" then moved to Groveton and set up a defensive position along an unfinished railroad. Longstreet followed Jackson's route to Groveton, leaving Anderson's Division behind to follow the next day if there were no enemy units on its front. Attacked by Pope on August 28, Jackson fought a tough defensive action, the Battle of Groveton. Over the next two days the Second Battle of Manassas, or Second Bull Run, was contested. Longstreet arrived to help Jackson on the evening of the August 29, and successfully assaulted Pope's left flank the following day. Anderson's Division—including the 14th Virginia in Armistead's Brigade— arrived at 3:00 a.m. following a punishing seventeen-mile march and, despite being held in reserve most of the day, pitched into the battle with enthusiasm at 4:45 p.m.[21] After his defeat Pope was able to retreat with most of his army.

Robert E. Lee then decided to invade the North. By his troops moving into Maryland, the Confederate commander hoped to win over that border state, draw Federal forces away from Virginia, and give Old Dominion farmers a respite from the war. Departing from Manassas on September 1, the 14th Virginia forded the Potomac River at White's Ferry on September 6, and marched into Frederick, Maryland, on September 8.[22] On September 9, Lee detached Jackson's II Corps—along with elements of Anderson's Division, including the 14th Virginia— to seize Harpers Ferry, as well as its garrison, in order to eliminate the threat they posed to his supply lines.[23] While Southern forces gained the heights surrounding Harpers Ferry, the 14th Virginia guarded a road leading to Sandy Hook, Maryland. At daybreak on September 15, Jackson's artillery began firing down into Harpers Ferry, causing the 12,000-man Federal garrison to surrender at about 8:00 a.m.[24] Following this victory the Confederates at Harpers Ferry, including the 14th Virginia, were force-marched to Sharpsburg, Maryland, to join Lee in the vicious battle being fought there. There the regiment was hurried into battle line, but the fighting had already ended.

Lee's Army of Northern Virginia faced about and started back across the Potomac River on September 19. That day the 14th Virginia crossed the river, and—while covering the army's retreat—reached Martinsburg that evening. Eventually the unit marched further south to Winchester where it went into camp.[25] On October 30, 1862, the 14th Virginia departed Winchester and, tramping through Front Royal, arrived in Culpeper, Virginia on November 2.

It was while the regiment was in Culpeper that Merit wrote the following letter to Jane. Evidently a letter of hers had caught up with him there. In it she must have claimed that Merit had forgotten her. (After his release from the hospital—unfortunately, we do not know the date—he must have been marching almost every day, and possibly saw some action, so he may not have had the opportunity to write. It was certainly a long, letterless gap from August 1 to November 11, 1862, and it was unlike Merit to go so long without writing. He may not have written to his sweetheart during this period of extreme army activity—but it's just as likely that his letters just never went through.)

Culpeper court house
November the 11th 1862
Dear Rosser   I take my pen in hand to write you a few lines

*to let you know I am well   I Received your letter a few days
ago and I was truly glad to hear from you   I am sorry that
you think I have forgot about you but I don't blame you for
saying so   I knew I aught to com to se you before now but
I could not com without I Run the blockhead and I didnt
like to do that   I liked to act onerable if I can   If I had
pretended to sick to keep out of battle and com home that
day I might bin there long ago but think myself above that
you may look for me soon   I will be there between now and
chrismas som time   I may com in two or three weeks and I
may com sooner   I am certainly coming before chrismas   I
cant get any ferlow but I am coming any how   you will hear
from me before I get there   you need not write any more   yet
if you do you must Right to gordensville   we will be there
before long   nothing more
yours sencearly
M B Thurman*

While the 14th Virginia was in Culpeper, Armistead's
Brigade was assigned to Maj. Gen. George E. Pickett's Division in
Longstreet's I Corps.[26] They stayed in Culpeper until November
20, when they started for Fredericksburg with Longstreet.[27]
When the following missive was written—it's not clear whether
it reads "19th" or "14th"—Merit evidently already knew that
this movement was planned and that it would take him further
away from Fluvanna County. He wrote to Jane, therefore, that
he was definitely coming as he had promised in his previous
correspondence. To this letter was attached a page on which he
had practiced writing "Jane R thurman" a number of times. It's
hard to make out the words below these except for "Gordonsville,
Va" and possibly "wife to be." It seems obvious from this extra
page (which is not included below), that Merit—the shy

boatman turned reluctant soldier—intended to marry Jane soon thereafter.

November The 19th 1862

MiSs Rosser   I take my pen in hand to write a few lines
to you to let you know I am well at the present time and
I hope when you receive those few lines it may find you
injoying the same blesings   I wrote you a few days ago that I
was coming between now and chrismas but you may look for
me in six or seven days if I am coming unless I stoped on the
way   I am going to Run the block head and com any how
know more at present   you may look for me   I certainly
coming   I will not disappoint you
Yours sencearly
M. B. Thurman
14th Va Regmt
Culpepeper C H.
Culpeper county Va

According to his service record, Merit made good on his promise to Jane by going absent without leave on November 22, 1862. He did not return to the 14th Virginia until December 20. Minister John Hall recited the marriage vows to Meredith "Merit" Branch Thurman and Jane Rosser Humphrey on December 2, 1862, in the Methodist Episcopal Church South at Union Mills in Fluvanna County. (According to a sign on the structure, the church was built in Union Mills for the mill workers in 1813. After the little Rivanna Canal village died, the church was moved to its modern location on Route 616, also known as Union Mills Road. Although Meredith's family nickname was "Merit," the marriage certificate spelled it

MARRIAGE LICENSE.

VIRGINIA—COUNTY OF *Fluvanna* TO WIT:

To any Person Licensed to Celebrate Marriages:

You are hereby authorized to join together in the Holy State of Matrimony, according to the rites and ceremonies of your Church, or religious denomination, and the laws of the Commonwealth of Virginia, *Mr. Merritt B. Thurman* and *Miss June R. Humphrey daughter of Mary Humphrey*

Given under my hand, as Clerk of the County Court of said County, this *2nd:* day of *December* 1862.

Abra: Shepherd, Jun. Clerk.

CERTIFICATE TO OBTAIN A MARRIAGE LICENSE,

To be annexed to the License, required by the Act passed 15th March 1861.

Time of Marriage, *2nd: December 1862*
Place of Marriage, *Union Mills*
Full Names of Parties married, *Merrill B. Thurman & Jane R. Humphrey*
Age of Husband, *Thirty seven years 29th: April last.*
Age of Wife, *about seventeen years*
Condition of Husband (widowed or single), *Single*
Condition of Wife (widowed or single), *ditto*
Place of Husband's Birth, *Chesterfield County Va.*
Place of Wife's Birth, *Fluvanna County Va.*
Place of Husband's Residence, *Same*
Place of Wife's Residence, *Fluvanna County Va.*
Names of Husband's Parents, *Hezekiah Thurman & Nancy M. Thurman*
Names of Wife's Parents, *Royal and Mary Humphrey*
Occupation of Husband, *Boatman*

Given under my hand this *2nd:* day of *December* 1862.

Abra: Shepherd j. Clerk.

MINISTER'S RETURN OF MARRIAGE.

I CERTIFY, that on the *2nd* day of *December* 1862 at *Union Mills* in *Fluvanna Co Va* I united in Marriage the above named and described parties, under authority of the annexed License. *Jn Hall Minister, M.E. Church South.*

☞ The Minister celebrating a Marriage is required, within ten days thereafter, to return the License to the Office of the Clerk who issued the same, with an endorsement thereon of the *fact* of such Marriage, and of the *time* and *place* of celebrating the same.

Merit and Jane's marriage license

"Merritt.") Jane's mother, Mary, had to authorize the marriage since her daughter was only seventeen years old. One of the witnesses, William L. Page, appears in some of Merit's letters and is married to one of Jane's older sisters named Irene. (The Mr. Richardson who helped Merit procure a passport to get back to the army is probably the Churchill "Church" Richardson mentioned in Susan Gillespie's letter to her husband, Jackson, who served in the Fluvanna Light Artillery.[28] Churchill Richardson is referred to as a neighbor.[29])

Permission by Jane's mother for Jane to marry Merit since she was only 17 years of age

During Merit's absence from his unit, the Battle of Fredericksburg was fought on December 13. As part of General Pickett's Division, Armistead's Brigade—including the 14th Virginia—held a portion of the Confederate center which was not assaulted by the Army of the Potomac under Gen. Ambrose E. Burnside. While heavy fighting raged to their left and right, Armistead's men were little more than spectators. Fredericksburg was a resounding victory for Confederate arms. Thus, when Merit returned to his unit, everyone was upbeat and glad to see him. Soon after he started the following letter of December 20, however, he was placed in the guardhouse.

Decb 20th 1862

Rosser my dear wife I have the oporturnity of writing afew lines to you to let you hear from me I am write well at the present time and when these few lines comes to hand I hope it may find you well I got hear yesterday saderday they have not put me in the gard house yet I don't know what they will do with me yet I dont expect they will do any thing with me they all seemed to be mighty glad to se me when I got back I didnt have any dificuly in geting to the army know one dident interfer with me in Richmond mr Richardson went with me up to the passport office I had no trublle in getting a pasport armistead's Brigade is Three mile this Side of Fredericksburg they are expecting another fight hear shortly but I don't expect I will fight any more I am going to try and get out of the army if the is any way to get out I want to be there with you and I intend to get there if the is any way to get there I love you now better then I ever did I thought I loved you before we was mariade is hard as I could but I love you better now then I ever did all the millintary laws in the Southern confedessy cant hold me hear but I wants to shun the laws and get of upon onerable terms is I can you must do all you can to get me off I spoke to mr Richardson about getting off he didnt Say whether he would or no but I think he will try and get me off I have know more news of importance to now it was Reported that captain poore was killed but it is not so armistead's brigade was not in the fight the is not any man hert in the brigade I havent any more to write this time

*you must write to me as soon is you can   I want to hear
from you   the is not much pleasure hear for me   I want to
Se you now worse then I ever did in my life   write soon and
I will write to you again   I have bin verry near dead evry
sence I left you   I think So much about you   I will now
bring my letter to close by saying I Remain your frend untell
death
Yours sencearly
M B Thurman
To Mrs Jane R Thurman
giv my best love to your mother
and all the famly   write me word how your
mother is and your sister also*

Four days later—on December 24, Christmas Eve—
Merit wrote again to his new bride. In this letter he told Jane that
he was in the guardhouse with 180 other men, including "Bobe
Holly" and "Alexander Forster." (The latter was actually James A.
"Foster," also of Company C, who went AWOL with Merit, but
returned to the 14th Virginia before he did). On the way back to
his company, Merit got to see his sister Mariah and his brother
Aurelious in Richmond. He also saw his brother Grandison and
his cousin, Beverly Ammonett. Merit's family was surprised to
hear that he got married—they thought he never would. In the
following letter Merit noted that a Yankee deserter who had
joined his brothers' infantry unit—Company D, 41st Virginia
Regiment—was an old acquaintance he had worked with in the
Chesterfield coal mines. Merit also included a message for Nat
who was AWOL.

*December The 24th 1862
    my dear wife   I now write you a few more lines to let*

44

*you hear from me   I wrote a letter to you the other day
that I was hear but they hadnt don any thing with me at
that time but they put me in the guard house the Same
day I started the letter to you   but you must not let your
feelings be hert about it   they cant hert me much   the is
one hundred and eighty is in the gard house beSides myself
Bobe holly is in the gard house and alexander forster the
one that went with me home   I dont know how long they
will keep me in the gard house but I intends to Run the
block head again and com to Se you before very long   the is
nothing can Stop me without it is death   I dont intend to
stay away from you at a time   I will all most Suffer death
for you   it most kills me to think I cant stay there with you
I love you so well   I love you better then I ever did   I never
will be contented Know more untel I can get there with you
to stay   if I thought I never would Se you again I know I
couldnt live long   my holl thoughts is about you   I would
Send for you to com downhear before long but the is no
place hear fit for a lady to com   we are out in the cold field
without any tents no more then what we make our Selves
and they don't allow any one to com down hear where
we is except them belongs to the army   they are expecting
another fight hear before long but they will not git me into
another fight   The smallpocks is in the army   all the men
is vaxenated I beleave   I am vaxenated my self   I Saw
my sister mariah and brother aurelious when I was in
richmond and brother Grandison and cuzon bevily amnet
I tole them I had the prettyest and the best wife in the world
they all wants to se you mighty bad   I could hardly make
them beliav it   they said I must bring you down so they
could Se you   they said they dident think I ever would get
married   they was verry much surpprised   the is a man in*

the company with my brothers that deserted from the yankey army at the fedricksburg fight   he is an old acquaintance of mine   my self and him worked to gether ten years ago at the chesterfield coal mines   burnsides got whiped badly at fedricksburg   our army killed and wounded 15 thousand yankeys So the Report says and we lost 4 thousand men they was not don burrying the yankeys when I got hear   I have no more news of importance this time   the is no pleasure hear for me   if I just could be with you I would be happy   the is only one thing that gives me any consolation that is I know I hav got you now and no boddy else can get you   I am going to try and get a discharge if I can   I think I can   I am working for it now   then I can com to dwell with the one who I love so dearly and well   tell nat not to let me perswade him to com   do what he things is best   I have tole him exactly what kirnal magruder said   fedricksburg is not burnt but the houses is tour all to peaces   three or four houses is burnt down   I dide hear any thing about your cuzon yet   Give my best lov to all your folks and write me word how your mother and Sister ellen is getting and don't let your feelings be hert about me being in the gard house all herts me becaus I cant be with you   I love you better then I do my Self   I will now bring my letter to a close by saying I will Remain your tru and affectionate frend untel death write as soon as you can
Yours Sencearly   M. B Thurman
14th Va Regment camp near Fredricksburg
In kear of captain R H poore

On December 28, 1862, the 14th Virginia marched from Fredericksburg to Guiney's Station in Caroline County for winter camp, a distance of about eight miles.[30]

Chapter 3 Endnotes

1   Crews and Parrish, p. 17.
2   Ibid., p. 17.
3   Crews and Parrish, p. 18.
4   Ibid.
5   Ibid., p. 19.
6   Ibid.
7   Ibid.
8   Ibid.
9   Ibid.
10   Charles W. Sublett, *57th Virginia Infantry* (Lynchburg, 1985), p. 47.
11   Crews and Parrish, p. 20
12   Ibid.
13   Ibid., p. 21–24.
14   Ibid., p. 24.
15   Wayne Motts, *Trust in God and Fear Nothing; Gen. Lewis A. Armistead, CSA* (Gettysburg, 1994), p. 40.
16   Crews and Parrish, p. 27.
17   Ibid.
18   Ibid., p. 28.
19   Ibid.
20   Ibid.
21   Ibid., p. 29.
22   Ibid., p. 30.
23   Ibid.
24   Ibid.
25   Ibid., p. 32.
26   Ibid., p. 33.
27   Ibid.
28   Ellen Miyagawa, ed., *Fluvanna History: Dear Susan* (Palmyra, VA, 2004), p. 47.
29   Ibid.
30   Hewitt, p. 35.

Chapter 4:
A Soldier Goes AWOL

Merit and the 14th Virginia Infantry began the new year—1863—in winter camp at Guiney's Station in Caroline County, about eight miles from Fredericksburg. They had been there since just after Christmas. Soon after his arrival at Guiney's Station, Merit penned a partial, undated letter to Jane. In it he mentioned the names of two other members of Company C—James Westcoat and Jesse Baltimore. (James Westcoat was discharged from the Richmond Hospital on December 27, 1862, and was present through June.[1] Jesse Baltimore was in camp and about to be detailed to the Petersburg Hospital on January 13, 1863.[2] From their records, therefore, and from what Merit said about one of them, this letter must have been written between December 27 and January 13. Despite his comment that he expected to go to North Carolina soon, the 14th Virginia was not ordered to North Carolina at this time—it must have been a rumor.)

Mr. Richardson had accompanied Merit to Richmond and had helped him get a passport back to his unit when he returned in December. Merit wrote that he had sent fifty dollars via Mr. Richardson and that he would send more later. According to Merit's record, he was paid on December 31, 1862. (Whether he received back pay at this time is not known. If he did, he could have dispatched it to his "prettyest and . . . best wife in the world" via Mr. Richardson. Another possibility is that Mr. Richardson made another visit in January as Merit received some socks from Jane via someone from home.)

Another man mentioned in this letter, John Walker, was evidently attempting to get Merit assigned to a boat. Perhaps Merit had worked for Walker on the James River and Kanawha Canal. In closing Merit asked Jane to send her letters "In Kear of Leutenant Thomas Morris." This was because his previous captain, Robert Poore, had been promoted to major in the regiment and Lieutenant Morris, who had led the company the last three months of 1862, was now officially in charge.[3] (Soldiers commonly had their mail directed to them via their commanding officer.) Unfortunately, the first part of the following letter is missing.

I supprised no time to Se me up there I have got so now I don't kear much which side hankers and as to john walkers geting me detailed to go to a boat I new that he couldentt do that at first but if I could just get out of the plaget war I would be independent of him or any other man I could get a boat my Self I wrote mr page a letter yesterday to come down and se me but you tell him to hold on untell I write to him again we have marching orders now we expects to go to goldsburrey norcralina in a day or two but I dont much expect to go my Self they are expecting a big fight jessee balltimoore is got his discharge jim wescoat is hear me and

*him stays together   me and him is good frends now more
then ever   I beleave I hav no more news of interest   give my
love to your mother and all the famly and also to Sister ellen
and mrs page and mr page   Know more at present   I Sent
you fifty dollars by mr Richardson and I will Send you Som
more the first conveniant opportunity Sencearly yours
M. B. Thurman
I will Remain your tru and affectionate
frend untel death   14th Regmt
Armisteds Brigade
Pickitts DiviSSion
In kear of Leutenant Thomas Morris
Write soon as you can*

It was while the 14th Virginia was still at Guiney's Station
that Merit wrote his next letter to Jane. A previous letter—one in
which he had mentioned "bill cambell" and "Tump smith"—may
be missing or, more likely, Jane wrote Merit about them insulting
her. Merit called "bill cambell" and "Tump smith" characters
that were not worth noticing. In the following Merit revealed his
frustration with the army—he had signed up for only one year
and they would not let him go home to his wife. He wanted out.

January the 16th 1863

*My dear good wife   I received your kind affectionate letter
this evening and I was very glad to hear from you   The is
nothing in this world afford me as much pleasure is to hear
from you   you are the greatest pleasure and comfort to me
in this world   This leaves me as well as common and I hope
when you receive these few lines it may find you injoying all
the blessings that god can afford you   oh if I could just be*

there with you it would such great pleasure to me I love you
so dearly that the will never be know more pleasure for me
untill I can get there to stay with you don't think anything
of me writing to you like I did I wanted to hear from you
so bad that I hardly new what to write I am sorry that
I mentioned anything about bill cambell I don't intend
to hav anything to do with him unless I am oblige to I
love you and it herts my felings to hear of any boddy saying
anything against you I wouldent do or say anything to hert
your felings my self and know one else shan't do it you is a
lady and I marriade you for a lady and I means to protect
you as long as I live and I means to do all I can to oblige
and comfort you know such carricters is bill cambell is not
worth noticing nor nether is Tump smith but I cant take
evrything I dont intend to truble him while I am in the
army I am trying to get out of the army all I can but they
are trying to hold me hear but I dont intend to do them
much good I am under arrest yet but not in the gard house
I hav not had my tryal yet you needent be
[Rest of letter not available]

In Merit's next letter—dated January 25, 1863—he
wrote how sorry he was to hear that Jane's mother was sick. He
was concerned as evidently she had been sick for some time. His
trial had not taken place, as yet, and he said that after his trial he
would try to get home. The regimental doctor had gotten Merit
permission to stay out of the guardhouse while he was awaiting
trial—he had free rein of the camp—as long as he promised not
to leave the company. He noted that if he were to go AWOL
again before his trial, it would be hard on him. Evidently he had
a medical problem involving his neck that he had had when he
was home with Jane while absent without leave. (It is not clear

whether it was a wound or the result of an accident.)

Another undated, partial letter perfectly continues the correspondence begun below—it also matches it in ink, paper, and contents as to Merit's circumstances—so it must be the second portion of the same letter. In the second piece Merit expressed how much he was missing Jane. Jane had sent him some socks to sell but, unfortunately, he did not get much for them as everyone seemed to have plenty. Nonetheless, he asked his loving wife for another pair. He also asked her to have two linen shirts made for him: He wanted to have them ready when he got home. Merit also told Jane to tell Miss Mary Morris that Dick—another Fluvanna County boy in Company C—"is Right well" and will write Mary soon.

Of special note is what Merit wrote concerning Lieut. Thomas Morris. Morris was acting very mean toward Merit and was doing all that he could against him. Evidently, the lieutenant did not want Merit to get off without punishment. (In Merit's next letter he instructed Jane not to direct any more correspondence in care of Lieut. Thomas Morris.) In the following Merit was still concerned about his brother-in-law, Nat Bacon, who was still AWOL from his company. (Bacon had married Jane's sister, Ellen, at Union Mills on April 20, 1857.) Merit also noted that sixty men were AWOL from the 9th Virginia Regiment of Armistead's Brigade and that the reward for their return was $1,800. Near the close he remarked that he would like to bring home a beau for Jane's sister, Caroline.

January the 25th 1863

My dear affectionate wife   I embrace the oppotunity of

*writeing a few lines to you this morning to let you hear
from me   I am well at the present time and I truly hope
when these few lines comes to hand they may find you well
and injoying all the blessings and comfort that god can
afford you   I Received your kind and affectionate letter
day before yesterday which I was exceedingly glad to hear
from you   nothing can afford me as much pleasure without
I could se you   I am verry Sorry to hear that your mother
is so sick   I wish it was so that I could be there so as I could
do something for her   anything she wants you must get
it for her and charge it to me   that is all I can do   I cant
come home yet   I have not had my Tryal yet and if I was
to go home before I had my Tryal it would make it hard
on me   I am not in the gard house now   I go anywhere in
camp that I want to go   they cant do but verry little with
me but I am bound to stand a Tryal accordng to law   as
soon is that is over I will try and come home again   I am
coming if I am killed for it   I woulden't give you for all the
Southern states   you said that you had rather be punished
your self then for me to be punished but you shall never be
punished on my account if I can help it tho it makes me love
you better to think that you are willing to be punished for
me   I am willing to do anything in the world for you that
lies in my power   I would suffer death for you   it seems
from your letter that you think that I am punished but I
have not had any punishment yet and I dont expect to be
punished much   if I did I wouldent stay hear but I think
it is for the best   The doctor tole me that I could stay at the
Redgmt if I wouldent go away untel I had my tryal and I
promised him I wouldent   he took me out of the gard house
so is he could attend my neck   my neck is not any worse
then it was when I was there with you but I am trying to*

get off on the account of it   I would bin in the gard house evry since I have bin back hear if I hadent got the doctor to take me out   I am not confind   I dont have anything to do but I live a misrable life hear without you [End of first part of letter] and I know I never will se anymore pleasure without you   my tong cannot express my heart cannot tell how I feel when I think of the one that I love So dearly and well   you said in your letter that if I got sick I must send for you and you would come if I got sick   I will be sure to send for you and I want you to be Sure and come when I send for you   I would send for you to come down now but the is no place hear fit for you to come but if you was to come any how I would do the best I could for you   I want to se you worse then I ever did in my life   I have greived my self allmost to death about you som times   I am a great mind to go home and se you any how and let them do what they chose with in me   I never lived Such misrable life   before you said in your letter that I must write word how much I got for the socks you gave me   I only got one dollar and fifty cents a pare for them   the was so many socks in camp when I got hear I couldent get any more for them and you said you had a pare of briches for me   You had better keep them untel I com home   I hav got another pare since I got back   if you se a conveniant oppotunity you can send me a pare of socks   I hav two pare yet but I might want another pare   I want you to have me two linen bosam shirts made when you have the oppotunity   I want you to have them by the time I get home   you needent herry your Self about it and I will satesfy you for them   tel miss mary morris dick is a Right well   He Says he is going to write to her The first chance Tel nat and sister ellen they must write to me and let me no whether he is coming back or no   I expect I will be there

with him before long   I am going to try and get off by law
and if I cant get off that way I will get off any how   the is
60 men absent without leaf from the ninth Redgment   the
is 18 hundred dollars Reward for them   tel nat he must be
certain to write to me and you must write to me evry week
yourSelf   it is all the pleasure that I have iS Reading your
letters   Thomas morris is tryed to make against me all he
could   he is acted verry mean with me   he dont want me to
get off   he is bin talking about me to Som of the officers but
hiS word is nothing hear   he is thought but verry little of
hear in the company   I hope I will get out of this war onest
more and be a free man   then the day will be mine   I have
nothing more of importance to write at this time   tel miss
caroline I am going to carry her a beau when I come home if
she will accepet of him   giv my love to her and your mother
and all the family and tel mother she must make haste and
get well   I am geting uneasy about her being sick so long
you must write evry week   you must write me a long letter
my hole thoughts is about you   I hope you will not think any
the less of me for expressing my love so plain to you   I cant
help it   I dont expect I will come home untel march tho I
may come sooner   I hav nothing more to write at this time
I have only Received three letter from you   you must excuse
bad or Hard writeing
Yours Sencearly
M. B. Thurman To Mrs Jane R. Thurman
I yet Remains your sencear Husband
and will Remain   that is all I can Say   good by for this time
Direct your letters to the
14th Redgement Va Volentiars
ArmSteds Brigade
PickettS Division

In kear of Major R H Poore
Company C

Merit's next letter from Guiney's Station was undated but fits here in the chronology because Jane had told him that her mother was getting better. Also, Merit had received two letters from Jane the "day before yesterday" and one of them was dated January 20. This missive he may have received in mid February. Merit mentioned Jane's brother, Perrington—spelled "Purringon" in the 1850 Fluvanna County census—who was twenty-eight years old and asked that he come visit him in camp. Merit also mentioned that Mr. Richardson had visited recently and that he had sent forty more dollars home to Jane.

In the following Merit advised Mr. Page not to enter the Confederate service because his wife and children needed him at home. Then he told Nat, who was still AWOL, not to come back as it would be worse for him. Merit suggested instead that Nat try joining a cavalry unit. (It is interesting to note that Merit actually tried this tactic later on, while AWOL.) Merit also implied that Nat might try going over to the Union side and then send for his wife. (It's understandable that Merit had little good to say about service in the Confederate Army. After all, he had volunteered for one year and was being kept in the ranks—against his will—for almost another. Also, living out-of-doors and staying in unheated huts for this length of time is bad for anyone, especially considering what passed for winter clothing in 1862.) Merit hoped to come home in March, but if he could not, he said he may send for Jane. He probably hoped he could find private quarters for Jane nearby.

Guinny Station spottsylvania couty Va

*my own dear wife I embrace the oppotunity this evening
of writing a few lines to you to inform you that I am well
at this time and I truly hope from my heart when these
few lines coms to hand they may find you injoying all the
blessings that the world can afford you. I Received two
letters from you day before yesterday one was wrote the
20th of January I find out now that the letters dont come
Strate they are misplaced sometimes I had just wrote one
to send when I Received them two and I tore it up and I
had just written another today and I Received another I
tore that up and I will answer them all it makes me feel
Rejoyish when I get a letter from such a good frend and
one that I love and esteam So hyly my dear wife I hardly
know what to write to you I love you So good it most Ruins
me to think that I cant stay with you one who I love better
than any thing in the hold world I can Run the blockhead
and com home if I was a mine to do so but I have not had
my tryal yet if I did it would make it hard on me I am
walking about in the camp where ever I chose I am not
garded and I wanted to get off clear by law if I can then
the will be no more hear after but it iS hard for me to get
a discharge I dont want to Run the blockhead but I am
coming before long whether I get a discharge or no Tho I
know we all are bound to be governd by the laws or be put
to a great deal of trubble but I wouldent Stay away from
you and forsake you not for all the southern states nor I
wouldent give you for all the southern states and evrything
in it becaus I no I never would Se anymore pleasure without
you my pleasure would be Ruined if I did I am glad to
hear your mother is geting better I was getting verry uneasy*

about her   She is bin like a mother to me and She Shall
never Suffer for anything is long is I am able to help her
You must do the best you can for her and do the best you can
for your Self untel I come and I will be your frend untel I die
    dont direct your letters to tom morris no more   I thank
you kindly for the letter your brother wrote to me for you
and I thank him too   he is a gentleman every inch of him
he wrote it exactly iS I wanted it wrote   I wrote a letter
to your brother purinton yesterday   you must tell him to
come down and Se me   If he can come it will be a benefill
to him if his health will admit him to do So and if he wants
any money to get anything for me you must let him have
it and he can Return it to you when he goes back   he may
have the money and he may not but if he has not got it you
can let him have it   tel him to write me word when he is
coming   you said that you got the fifty dollars that I sent you
by mr. Richardson   he was down hear a few days ago and
I sent you forty dollars more   you said you rather I would
keep it my Self but I had rather that you should have it   I
will send you som more after a little while   make your Self
contented and do the best you can do for I am yours untel
death parts us   tel Mr. page to never come in the confederate
Service if the any way to keep out for the sake of his wife
and children and tel nat to never come hear now   I think
it will be worse for him   if I was clear of this war and was
there I would be a frend to him   I know he is bin a frend
to me   all the men in magruders company says if they was
in his place they would come back   tel him for god sake
not to let them catch him   I was in his place I would join
some calvery company untel I could get clear   I am fred he
will git caught   the is plenty of union people in virginia he
could get to and send for his wife   I no he will never se any

pleasure there   my dear good wife you may look for me in
march and if I dont com I will try and send for you   tel nat
I am going write him a letter in a few days and I will give
him all the news that I know   you must write to me as soon
as you git this   I will Bring my letter to a close by saying I
will Remain your tru and loving husband untel death parts
us   farewell for this time   Yours sencearly M B Thurman
to his dear loving wife Ms jane R. Thurman   14th Redgmt
kear of major R H poore

We now come to a break in Merit's letters to Jane. According to his service record, Merit went AWOL for the second time on February 17, 1863, while the 14th Virginia was on the march from Guiney's Station to Chester, Virginia, just south of Richmond. (Since the 14th Virginia left Guiney's Station on February 15 and reached Richmond four days later on February 19, Merit must have "hopped the fence" a little north of the Confederate capital.[4] There were several possible motivations. Merit knew that area very well and could visit his mother and brother Aurelious on his way home. Coincidently, his brother Robert—a member of Company D, 41st Virginia, of Brig. Gen. William Mahone's Brigade—was also visiting their mother while Merit was there. Leaving his hut in order to camp outside in the middle of winter was, perhaps, another motivation for Merit to go home, especially since nothing seemed to be happening in the war.) Merit returned to his company on March 13 and immediately penned a letter to Jane to advise her of his safe arrival. Merit told Jane that he was in the guardhouse, but did not expect to be there long. Jim Harlow, who was in Company H of the 57th Virginia, was in the guardhouse with him.[5]

Nat had been caught while at home and Merit searched for him through the pestilential Richmond prisons—Castle Thunder and Castle Lightning—so he could tell Ellen where he was and how he was doing. Merit inquired at the prisons' clerk's office and found that Nat's name was not on the list of prisoners. Merit hoped that Nat had escaped his captors. Since Merit used the word "again" in this regard, Nat must have managed an earlier escape, most likely from the Home Guards. Merit had left a picture of Jane with his mother—she "begged" him for it—but she also wanted her daughter-in-law to visit her in Richmond so our soldier scribe gave Jane directions. He was also hoping that his bride would visit him in camp.

march the 13th 1863

My dear loving good wife   I take pen in hand this evening to write to you onest more to let you hear from me   I have gotten back saft to the Army again   I am now in the gard house but I dont expect to be in the gard house but a few days   my dear Rosser make yourself contented the best you can and I will do the same   The best frends has to part som times   we cant be together all the time   I never had anything to hert me so bad is it did to part from you one who I loved so dearly   it is hard for me to part from such a good frend but I hope The Time will not be long before we will meat to never par again   the army is five mile below Petersburg but I dont know how long we will stay hear   I havent seen anything nor herd anything of nat yet   I went to cassle Thunder and cassle lightning both and inquired for him and he was neather place   I inquired at the clirkes office and his name is not on the book of the list of prisners and he is not at his Redgmt   I am in the hopes he iS got

away again you must write me word if you have herd
anything of him tel sister ellen to make her self contented
the best she can they will not do much with him becaus
they dident cach him going to the yankeys They caught
him at home I Stoped at Brother aureliouSes one day and
night brother Robert was there too he never got the letter I
wrote him he is not gone to the army yet mother and all of
them sends there love to you and says you must be sure and
come down and Se them I let mother have your likeness
the old woman begged me so hard for it I thought I would
let her have it for a while if you come down you must go to
the Army bridge and inquire for mr. mahones and he will
till you where aureliouS iS working so you can Se him but
I Recon you had better weight untell I write to you again
before you come down and I will try and arrange it and so
you can come and se me too if I can tel your sister I will do
all I can for nat if he comes down hear jim harlow is in the
gard house with me excuse me for my short letter nothing
more at present
yours sencearly M. B Thurman Remains your frend untel
death
camp near Petersburg Picketts divisions armsteds
Brigade Rite soon as you can I love you so dearly

When Merit returned to his company he was placed in
the guard house, and quickly discovered that brother-in-law Nat
was confined there as well. Attached to the bottom of Merit's
letter—on the same sheet of paper—was a note from Nat ("N. D.
Bacon") to his mother-in-law, Mrs. Mary Jane Humphrey, Jane's
mother. In it Nat advised her to send her letters to "Thurman,"
meaning Merit, as he could get them best that way.

61

Camp near peterSburg
March the 17th 1863
Dear mother   I write a few lines to you as I hav the
oppotunity to inform you that I am well at the present time
I have gotten back to the army Safte without any diferculty
I was put in the gard house for five days but I am now clear
and Released from the gard house   nat is hear in the gard
house   he got hear yesterday   He stayed in cassle thunder
6 days   I inquirerd at cassle thunder and cassle lightning
when I was there but the Reson I dident hav his right name
I dont know what they will do with him yet   nat Seeme
to be verry uneasy about his wife and children   he Says he
dont kear so much about him Self if it was not for them   I
havent any more of importance to write this time   nat wrote
a few lines him Self   give my love and Respects to all your
family and Receive a good potion of it for your Self   I will
now bring my letter to a close by Saying I still Remains your
affectionate Son untel death
yours Sencearly
M. B. Thurman to Mrs M J Humphrey
camp near petersburg
14th va Redgmt
Armisteads Brigade
Picketts division / to M. J. Humphrey

Dear Mother   I drop you a few lines to let you know that I
am well and hope these few lines may find you enjoying all
the Blessings and comforte life can afford   I am in the guard
House & Dont no what will Be Done with me But I hope
not much   give my love to all the family & also Wms family
and all enquiring friends and Receive a large Portion for
your Self   nothing more   But Remain your affate Son ever

more   N. D. Bacon   Direct your letters to Thurman as he
can get it the Best   Good bye

The 14th Virginia was now near Petersburg, Virginia.
Merit noted in the following that he was no longer in the
guardhouse, having stayed there only five days. He did not
mention anything about his neck, so perhaps it was better after
his time at home with Jane. (Much could be said about a soldier
returning to his company voluntarily after staying away for less
than a month.) The officer who had been so hard on Merit in
December, Lieut. Thomas Morris, went on leave March 13 and
was not there this time to work against him.[6]

Nat Bacon and Jim Harlow were still in the guardhouse—
Merit and Nat had been there together for one day. Nat Bacon
and Jim Harlow's regiment—the 57th Virginia, Armistead's
Brigade—was about twenty miles away and its prisoners
had been left in the brigade camp. Merit visited Nat in the
guardhouse every day, and did not think "they will do much with
him," but was uncertain whether his brother-in-law would again
absent himself without leave. Merit was discouraged about the
course of the war and did not believe the South would win. Merit
was also concerned about the soldiers' families suffering at home
while other people were "living at home in splendor . . . starving
the poor ones." (It was a sad time for the soldiers' families—no
wonder so many men went AWOL.) Merit told Jane that if
everything went well, he would send for her after May 10.

march 21, 1863

My dear RoSser   I with he greatest of pleasure seat myself
this morning to write to you to answer your letter which

63

I Received yesterday and nothing cant afford me as much pleasure is to hear from one that I love so dearly and esteam so highly iS I do you   I am well at this time and I truly hope and trust from heart when these few lines comes to hand that they might find you injoying all the blessing and comfort that this world can afford you   it is all the pleasure I hav her is to read your kind and affectionate letters   what a happy man I would be if i could just liv there with you the one who I love so dearly is I do love you   I am a little better satesfied then I was when I left you before becaus I know we cant stay together all the time The way times is now   we must do the best we can and live in hopes for better times whitch I am in hopes that will not be long   I am not in the gard house now   I only stayed in the gard house five days and I was releasd from the gard house   I am clear now   I dont think they will do any more with me then take my pay for the time I was at home and I dont kear much for that   I am coming to se you again after a while if I am killed for it   I am willing to die for you   I know I couldent die in a better caus becaus I know the never would be no more peace for me if I never could se you for you are all my thoughts night and day   I havent much news to write this time   I want you to make your self contented the best you can and dont greave no more then you can help   I know you are so tender hearted tho I cannot help from greaving my self   Jim harlow is in the gard house yet   my self and nat stayed in the gard house one day together   I go to se him at the gard house every day   he seame to be toleble will contented   he can get away if he choses but I dont think they will do much with him   I dont know whether he intends to way yet or not   he is got plenty chance if he will   I havent seen kirnal maygruder yet   his redgmt is about twenty mile from us   I

64

*expect they will be back hear in a few days   all the prisners
from the 57th is left hear and sum few men to take kear of
the things at the camp   we may move way from hear but I
dont know yet if we stay hear   I will try and send for you
to come down hear about the tenth of may   we are now
about 4 mile below Petersburg   the is no fighting going on
hear now but they are be expecting fighting before long   I
hav less opinion of the south now then I ever did   I think
the north will whip   I dont se much chance for the South
without to konker the north without them men that is there
Riding about after there own men and them that is got
subsitutes will com and help   I think all the men is getting
disheartened and it is a nough to dishearten any boddy to
think how poor men has to suffer hear and there familys
suffering at home and greaving them selves to death   a
great many of them and others living at home in splendor
and spectulating starving the poor ones   I havent any more
news of importance   you must write to me as soon is you
can   tell sister ellen not to greav about nat no more then she
can help   I dont think they will be much don with him   I
wouldent be surprised if he want back there before long   I
will now bring my bad letter to a close by saying I Remain
your tru affectionate frend and Husband untel death parts us
Yours sencearly
M. B. Thurman To Mrs Jane R Thurman write soon as you can*

Eight days after writing his last letter to Jane, Merit
penned another as his company had just arrived at Ivor Station
southeast of Petersburg (about seven miles below present-day
Wakefield, Virginia.) Generally, when the army was on the
march, Merit did not get many chances to write. When the 14th
Virginia stayed at one location for a few days, however, he often

took pen in hand. In the following he observed that Jane's letters had not caught up with him. These messages from home meant so much to Merit—they were his only connection to his young wife. She was all he could think about. Merit expressed his doubts about God in this letter.

In the March 29 letter Merit noted that, as yet, he had not been tried for going AWOL in February. He was afraid the trial "will go hard with him." He was thinking about going AWOL again—before the trial—but only if Jane would consent. He evidently believed Nat was leaving and he was thinking of going with him. Merit wrote that they had been wading through swamps over their knees, so it would be difficult for Jane to visit. When Nat sent for Jane's sister, Ellen, to come, however, Merit wrote that Jane should come with her. (Evidently the two young ladies could assist each other through the swamps.) Merit's mother really wanted her daughter-in-law to visit her in Richmond, so Merit gave Jane instructions involving asking for his brother, Aurelious, at the army bridge over the James River. (Aurelious, no doubt, would direct her to Merit's mother.) Merit also mentioned that he had a Yankee jacket and other things he wished to send home with her.

Merit included a beautiful love poem to Jane in this letter. This was the second poem he had written for her. Finally, Merit decided not to go AWOL again, because if he did he would not receive the over one hundred dollars owed him and he wanted to send that money to Jane. Merit and Nat were perhaps planning to go somewhere other than Fluvanna County—some place safe— and send for their wives when they got there. In a postscript, Merit sent his love and respects to Mr. and Mrs. Page.

march the 29th, 1863

*My dear loving affectionate wife   I embrace the oppotunity
of writeing a few more lines to you to let you hear from me
I am right well at the present and I truly hope when you
Receive these few lines this may find you well and injoying
all The blessings and comfort that god can afford you in This
world   I hav not Received but one letter from you Sence I
got back to the army the last time but I know your letter
haS not had time to ge hear yet.   The army is now forty
mile below petersburg on black water River at Ivoir station
the is a Talk of A big fight down hear verry soon   my dear
Rosser I Think more of you and I love you better then I
ever did in my life   you are on my mind all the time bothe
day and night   It herts my feelings So bad To Think I am
situated So That I cant do for you and Treat you as good
is I ought To Treat you but I hope and Trust The time will
not be long before I will be free again   The iS nothing in
this world can afford me any pleasure and make me happy
but my dear wife that I lov So dearly   you are all I liv for
in ThiS world   without you I would be misrable all the
balance of my days and with you I would I would be happy
I hope and trust if the iS a just god he will spare uS to come
to gether So iS we can liv happy my dear Rosser   I hav had
one tryal for going home the first time but I dont no what
will be don with me yet   I hav got to have another Tryal
yet for going home the last time which I expect will go hard
with me if I stand the Tryal but I dont think I will   I may
go with nat but I dont want to go without you are willing
but I think it iS for the best   but I will not go without your
conSent unless I am most oblige to go   I would send for you
to come down hear but the is no way for you to get hear*

we had to wade threw Swamps over our neeS to get hear
where we are now   if I do go with nat you must do the best
you can untel I come back again and if you dont hear from
me make your Self content   I will Send for you when nat
Sends for Sister ellen and I want you to be Sure and come
without fail   You must write on to me aS Soon iS you can
and let me no whether you are willing or no   I will not do
anything against your will nor without your consent becaus
I no you wouldent advise me to do anything no not to do
anything without you thought it was for the best   you must
come down and Se mother the first chance you have   She
wants to Se you mighty bad   you and Sister ellen both must
come   inquire for brother aureliouS at the armry bridge
at the confederate Army   he works There   you will be sure
to find him there   don't tel mother nor no boddy that I am
going and you can tell your mother when you come down
to Richmond to Se mother I hav got a yankee jacket and
Some more things there I want you to Send home or carry
Them when you go back and keep Them untell I come back
I will come back except I die   the is nothing will prevent me
without it is death becaus I lov you better then evrything
in this world and I will do anything for you that ever iS in
my power becaus I beleave I hav got the best wife in thiS
world   you are good enough for me   I dont want you to be
no better then you iS   I am mighty Sorry I hert your feelings
So at buck island that night   it herts my feelingS evry time
I Think about it   I havent any more news to write now   giv
mother my best lov amd give miSs caroline my best lov and
miSS juliar and all your sisters and to all your frends
Think of me when I am fare away and I will Think of the
evry hour in the day   I will Remember my Tru loving wife
That I left behind becaus you are only one that ever could

*Soot my mind   my heart iS now in greaf and pain but yet
I hope the time will come that we will meat to never part
again   you must write iS Soon is you can and if you don't
get an answer you may no where I am   I hav got about one
hundred and 25 dollars oweing to me yet   I would like to
get that and Send it to you if I could but be I cant get it yet
and if I was to go way I dont expect They would pay it to
you   but no matter where I go I will come back to you again
and will be your frend   nothing more at present   fare you
well for a while   I will ever Remain your tru affectionate
Husband untel death   Merit B Thurman   it iS hard for
frends to part but we are bound to part Some Times
ivoir Station South Hamton county Va
14th Va Redgmt
Armisteads Brigade
Pickets Division
give Mr Page and MrS Page my Best love and RespectS*

The next extant letter from Merit to Jane was dated
"Aprel the 25th 1863," leaving a gap of almost a month. (Merit
noted in it, however, that he had written her a few days earlier.
This letter, unfortunately, is missing—possibly for the reasons I
cited earlier.) Merit's company had been out on picket duty and
had skirmished with Union troops since leaving Ivor Station for
the Suffolk area on April 9.[7] The company was absent from the
brigade in Isle of Wight County—doing reconnaissance—for
two days during the period of April 10 through 30.[8]

During this period—April 11 through early May,
1863—General Pickett's Division participated in the
Confederate siege of Suffolk, Virginia, being held by Union
forces. On April 24, 1863, the enemy advanced in force from his

works before Suffolk and attacked the 14th Virginia, but were driven back by the unit's picket line.[9] Merit reported that during the picket fight he was in a great deal of danger—cannon balls and bullets whistling all around him. He wondered if his time had come and thought he might not see his wife again. In the fight, wrote Merit, Captain Poindexter and Captain Tompkins were killed, and Captain Chappell was wounded. (According to the regimental report, however, Captain Tompkins and Captain Poindexter were both wounded with Tompkins dying later.[10]) Merit noted that the 57th Virginia was also in the action, but were behind breastworks and thus suffered no casualties.

General Armistead's purpose in the Suffolk area, according to Merit, was to keep the Yankees contained in the city while his brigade foraged in the surrounding area. Merit remarked that some captured Yankee prisoners said they were going to starve the Southerners out. He tended to believe it—Merit and his comrades-in-arms only got enough to eat when they bought it themselves. From what Merit wrote, the money owed him was the only thing keeping him in the army. Merit remarked that he may start home on May 10, the second anniversary of his one-year enlistment. He noted that all of the bridges were guarded, however, so he could not get away. He also asked Jane to continue trying to get him assigned to a government boat.

Merit also added the following message for Ellen; according to a soldier in Nat's regiment named "harris jineny," her previous two letters to Nat were opened by Capt. Ralph Lewis Rogers. ("Jineny" may be Isaac Janney of Company A of the 57th Virginia.[11])

nancymond county Virginia
Aprel the 25th 1863

My Dear wife   I seat my Self to write to you onest more as
I hav an oppotunity though I wrote a letter to you a few
days ago but I will write to you evry chance I have   if I put
it off I may not hav another oppotunity   I am well all to a
little Rumatism in my left shoulder   I sincearly hope when
these few lines comes to hand they may find you well and
injoying all the happynesS that this world can afford you
in this life   we are now in four mile of suffolk   we got into
a pickit fight in the woods last Friday the day I started the
last letter to you and two of our best captains in the 14th
Redgment got killed and one wounded   captain parke
pondexter from chesterfield county was killed and captain
thomkins from Bedford county waS killed and captain
chappel from amealia county slitity wounded   none the
Rest in the 14th was not hert but we was in a great deal of
danger   the canon balls and bullets was whisling all around
us   I dident know what minute that my time would come
I thought to my Self at the time the fighting was going on
that I would giv evry thing in the world to Se you if I had
it and I wonderd if I ever would Se my dear pretty wife any
more   my dear Rosser you dont know how bad it herts my
feelings to think as dearly iS I lov you then cant stay with
you   it looks like Som times I cant stand staying away from
you so long it greaves me most to death but I hope they will
be pleasure for us yet before we die   we must live in hopes if
we die in dispare   times is hard hear   the 57th Redgment
was in the fight too but none of them dident get hert   they
was at another place behind brestworks   they killed Right
smart of the yankeys   we are looking for a big fight now in

71

*a few days but I hope it will not be   they are not trying to
take suffolk now but they are trying to keep the yankeys in
suffolk untel they can hall all the farrage from Round about
the country hear above black water   we took five yankey
prisners   they say they think they can starve us out and I
beleave so too for we don't get much more then half enough
to eat hear without we by it ourselves   my dear wife and
frend I call you my frend becaus I know you is my frend
and I dont intend to stay hear long   I will try and stay
hear untel I draw my money and if I stay untel then I will
try and come home if I can and if I dont come home I will
Sind you the money and I will go where I think I can make
more then I can hear   it may be a long time before I se you
but when I do se you I hope I will hav something for you   I
may start home about the tenth of may but I dont know yet
becaus I dont know is I can get there   we are in a mighty
bad place hear to get home   we are Right between the
dismal swamp and the black water River and evry bridge
and place where a man can cross iS garded   my sweet loving
wife if it Should happen so that I dont come home you must
try and do the best you can untel I can Se you again   god
knows I lov you better then evry thing in this world and the
is nothing in this world that I can do for you but what I will
do if it is in my power and with the greatest pleasure   I do
hope and that god will spare us to come together onest more
and so is we can liv happy together   I know the is nothing
in this world can make me liv happy but you   you must try
and do all you can to get me on the government boat and if
you cant pleas let me know as soon is you can becaus I don't
intend to stay hear   if I could just get there with you how
glad I would be   if I should go away I will come to you as
soon is I can and if I cant get to you I will try and send for*

you to com to me and you must come if you can the never
was such time sence this is bin a world before and I hope
peace will soon be made and then the never will be such
times know more giv my best lov to mother and all the
famly I will write Sister Ellen a letter in a few days tel
Sister ellen capt Rodgues broke open both of them letters so
harris jineny told me I havent seen him yet he is out on
pickit I will se him in a few days I herd he said nat owed
som money in camp and he was going to pay it with that
money know more at present dont send me no money
keep it for you self may god bless you forever I Remain
your tru frend and husband untel death parts us from this
unfrendly world Merit B Thurman to
Mrs jane R Thurman my loving wife
[At top of second page of letter is: "direct your letter to
petersburg 14h virginia Redgment."]

Just four days after his last letter to Jane, Merit wrote the
following to his brother-in-law, Nat Bacon, who was then AWOL.
A few days earlier Merit had received a letter from Nat in which
he announced that he had arrived home safely. (In other words,
Nat had not been caught during the journey.) From what Merit
wrote in his letter, he had helped Nat escape into the pines. Tump
Shepard—5th Sergeant of Company A, 57th Virginia—thought
he saw Merit and Nat go into the woods but did not see Nat come
back out. (Perhaps Merit was on guard duty at the time and used
the opportunity to assist his brother-in-law.) Fortunately for Merit,
Sergeant Shepard could not be sure of what happened, so nothing
came of it other than Col. John B. Magruder asking him where Nat
had gone. Merit lied and said he did not know anything about Nat,
and imagined that he had gone over to the Yankees. Merit wrote
that given the chance, he would help Nat go AWOL again.

Merit mentioned to Nat Bacon that he was home for ten days, a fact which perhaps explains a gap in the letter sequence. (There is nothing in Merit's service record about his being AWOL during this period, so perhaps he was on leave.) While Merit was gone—from April 11 through 20—the 14th Virginia had been probing the Federal defensive positions and found them too strong to assail.[12] Merit noted that a few days after his return, on April 24, the 14th Virginia was in a fight in which both Captains Poindexter and Tompkins were killed. (This was a heavy skirmish on the Edenton Road outside of Suffolk. When writing to Nat, Merit was more specific as to the way the two captains were hit. He must not have wanted to worry Jane with the gory details.) Merit remarked that no one else in the 14th Virginia was injured in the combat, which was fortunate, and that the 57th Virginia was behind works and had nobody killed or seriously wounded.

Merit reported that two Confederates ran over to the Yankees during the skirmish. He also noted that many Southerners had deserted while they were in the Suffolk area. Merit was thinking of either deserting or going AWOL, but all of the bridges were guarded and it was difficult to leave. (It appears that, in that marshy region of southeastern Virginia, those Confederates posted at bridges had to be wary of people approaching from both the front and the rear.) At this time Merit was still waiting for his back pay, perhaps the only thing keeping him with his company. If he did "go missing," he wrote, Ellen or Jane should write to Pvt. Samuel Kirtley—a member of Company C who taught school before the war—and he would write Nat as to his whereabouts.[13] (Evidently, Private Kirtley was a close friend and could be trusted.)

Merit remarked that their mission around Suffolk was to forage for food. With two armies in the area, however, he worried about what the civilians were going to eat. Evidently, when the Confederate forces vacated Suffolk, the Federals who moved into the void assisted the locals and there may have been more food. With the Confederate Army back in the area, however, and the Federal troops confined to the city, provisions were scarce. Food prices had gone up substantially, and Merit quoted prices for bacon, soap, and salt to prove his point. As he had mentioned in his previous letter to Jane, he had to buy himself food as the Confederate Army was not issuing enough.

The entire war-time situation Merit found disgusting. His letters to Jane were being opened and if he tried to go home, the Home Guards would chase him and probably capture him. On top of that the Home Guards—whom he called "scamps"—were worse than the Yankees. Additionally, there were "Rich men Riding about there taking pleasure and speculating and doing as they pleas" (by which he may have meant taking pleasure with women). All of this was happening while the poor soldiers were getting starved and killed to save the rich men's Negroes.

Merit was also upset that Capt. Ralph L. Rogers—who commanded Company H, 57th Virginia—had opened two of Ellen's letters to Nat. Ten dollars, which must have been in one of the letters, Merit had intended to give to another soldier to whom Nat owed money. That soldier was identified as Bill Thompson, the 1st lieutenant in Company H, Nat's company.[14] Merit went to regimental headquarters and asked for the letters, but was told that Captain Rogers had them and he was in the woods on picket duty. Thomas Mayo told Merit that he did not think Captain Rogers would cough them up. (There *was* a James Mayo in Company H who was probably a private and doctor's assistant—Thomas P. Mayo—who was also listed in the 3rd Virginia.[15]) So Merit told Nat to get Ellen to write Captain Rogers, telling him to hand over the money. In this letter Merit revealed much of how he felt about the war.

Aprel the 29th 1863

Mr. Bacon dear friend I hav the opotunity to Write a few lines to you to inform you that I am well at present and hopes when these few lines come to hand they may find you injoying the Same blessings I got your letter a few days ago which I was exceedingly glad to hear from you and to hear you went Saft you are Saft now and dont never let them have the pleasure of bringing you back no more I Stayed there behind ten days my Self I thought all the Fighting would be over before I came up to the Redgment and I hadent bin hear but two days before I got in to a fight we are in the woods on pickit and the yankeys advanced on us from there fortyfycations with both artelry and infantry we had hot times of it for two hours and we had two of our best captainS in the fourteenth Redgment killed and one wounded captain pondexter was from chesterfield county was killed and captain thomkins from bedford was killed had both legs shot of above his nees with a canon ball captain pondexter had Six balls put in him captain chappel was slitely wounded none of the Resr in the 14th didentget hert the was a good many yankeys killed more than they was of ours the 57th was engaged in the fight too at the same time they was about two mile from us they behind works Some few of them was shocked by the canon balls but none killed or seriously wounded they are

expecting another big fight hear in a Short time but I hope
it will not be two men Run over to the yankeys from the
57th while they was fighting and one yankey came over our
Side a good many of our men is gone to the yankeys since
the army is bin down hear and a good many more iS talking
about going nat I will try and do what I promised you if
I can we are now between the black water and the dismal
Swamp and the gards is at evry place on the black water
that a man can croSS I dont know whether I can get home
or know but I will try and if I dont I will go the other side
and I will expect for you to meat me on the other Side timS
is hard hear the citerson about hear in the neigborhood
says they lived well before the Southern army came hear but
Since they Run the yankeyS in times is hard they could get
best bacon for 15 pen lbs at eight and ten dollars Soap 25
cents a abare Salt 3 dollars Sack and evry thing else cheap
according If I Should be missing you can get Lister elen or
Ross to Rite to Samuel C. Kirtly and he will write to you
where I am he is all write he is an intermit frend of mine
I want to get what money I can and Send it to Rosser I
want her to hav it it will not do me any good and if it did
I Rather for he to hav it becaus I can make out without
it I forgot to mention in the above the yankeys took a hole
battery from genral hoods division last week and three
hundred men they Say now they dont want to take Suffolk
they just want to keep the yankeyS in suffolk untel they can
hall all the forrage from about over above black water then
after they do that what iS the peple a going to do about hear
I heard Som of the poure people Say when we vacuated
Suffolk before they would Starved if the yankey hadent help
them The Rich people is coming the day now but I hope
the day will be ours before very long I dont intend to stay

77

hear   I dont want to forsake my wife and I havt intend but I cant do any good hear   I cant stay with her and I cant go tose her and cant write to her without the letters being broke open and Read and when I do go home I have to Run away and go and then I am Ran of by packs of scamps with there guns and pistols   they are wors then yankeys and the Rich men Riding about there taking pleasure and speckulating and doing as they pleas and the poure men geting killed and starving to save their negroes   I know I can make a living without Staying hear and I dont intend to Stay if I can get away   I know I can do a great deal better then I can hear and I will come home if I can and if I don't come home I will go the other way and Send for Ross when times get so I can send for her if she will come that iS if I dont come back to old fluvanna again   I think virginia will be vacated before long   I saw kirnal magruder day before yesterday   he asked me where you was.   I tole him I dident know anything about you   I expect you was gone to the yankeys   he dident Say anymore to me   I went on to the 57th Redgement and ask for the letters that Sister Ellen sent to you and they said capt Rodgers had them and had broke them open and read them and had the ten dollars and thomas mayo said he dident think Rodgers would give it to me   he said you was oweing bill thomson Something and he beleav Rodgers is going to pay it to him   Rodgers iS in the woods on pickit   I havent Seen him yet   I Recon I will se him in a day or too   you Sister elen had better Rite an order to captain Rogers to pay it to me and I may get it   he has no write to pay it any boddy without an order from her he is got no rite to pay it to bill thomson nor no boddy else without an order from her   they tryed verry hard to get me in a Scrape about his going away but they couldent get profe

Sufficiant Tump Shepard Said he Saw you come out in the
pines with me and he dident Se you any more after that and
he beleaved I smuggled you off but beleaving So wouldent
do he had to know it and I was know gard what I dun I
will do it again and I will do more then that I hav no more
of importance you must write Soon as you can I will try
and come home if I can nothing more but yet Remains
your tru frend and brother untel death
yours Respectfully
M. B. Thurman Petersburg Virginia
14th Virginia Redgement Armisteads Brigade
Pickits division dont you go way untel you
know I am gone I wil come home if I posably can

On April 29, 1863, Lee ordered General Longstreet to join him near Fredericksburg. By the time "Old Pete" got moving on May 4, however, the Battle of Chancellorsville was already being fought. Longstreet's force—which included Pickett's Division and a division under Maj. Gen. John Bell Hood—marched 115 miles to Falling Creek by April 10. Merit and the men of 14th Virginia were now only about nine miles south of Richmond. Merit, therefore, saw this as an opportunity for Jane to visit his mother and possibly also see him. In the following letter he gave her specific directions on how to find his mother and himself. Merit also talked about a hurried letter he had written her (which may be missing, or perhaps the one dated April 25). Merit was upset to hear that Jane was afraid for him to return to Fluvanna. She had heard that "they"—probably meaning the Home Guards—had announced that they would shoot all the men who came home (referring, of course, to deserters and those absent without leave). He said he was not afraid of them, and called them cowards. Once home, he noted, he would shoot back if they interfered.

George Madison of Company F of the 19th Virginia told Merit that he heard that Caroline, one of Jane's sisters, was dead as well as "one of the mis fillmores."[16] Merit responded that there was nothing to it. (Perhaps George was a beau of Caroline's as Merit mentioned in one letter that he would "carry" her one. At any rate, George was very uneasy about Caroline.)

Merit obviously had access to newspapers as he reported in the following letter of May 10 that the papers said "general jackson died yesterday at three oclock." (After being wounded by his own men at Chancellorsville, Jackson had died of pneumonia.) He also noted that Thomas Seay—an eighteen-year-old private in his company—and some others had gone over to the enemy.[17] (Merit called the other deserters "nienks"—that is, if the word was transcribed correctly. Perhaps he meant "sneaks" or perhaps "nienks" was a fellow soldier's nickname.)

may 10th, 1863.

My Dear Wife I take my pen in hand to write a few lines to you onest more as we hav not left chesterfield yet   the army is now in nine miles of Richmond on the petersburg Railroad near falling creek.   I want you to come down to Richmond and you can go to brother Aureliouses and Se mother and all of them and aurelious will come with you out where I am or he will get som boddy to come with you you can come down on the central Railroad and you can inquire for the confederate army and you will find aurelious there and if he is not there you inquire for mr mahones on the corner of fifth and bird street and they will Sho you where aurelious lives   we are right on the Railroad and you will not hav any where to walk   inquire for the 14th

*Redgmt pickits division armisteads Brigade and you will find
me get aurelious to find out where pickits division is before
you leave Richmond becaus we may leave hear before you get
down hear come as soon as is you can dont put it off the
last letter I wrote to you I wrote it in a herry I didnt write all
I intended you wrote to me is if you was fraid for me to come
home you said they said they was going to shoot all the men
that come home but when I come I am coming prepard to
shoot some of them too you need not be fred of me geting shot
I hav had thousands of balls shot at me sence I saw you if the
men up there was so brave why dident they shoot the yankeys
when they came to fluvanna I am not afraid to come up
there when I get Reddy to come the is two or three up there I
means to hav a pull at if I liv I will never be satisfied untel I
get Revenge that is all I hav got to say about that now you
must come down as soon is you can I saw george maderson
to day he said he herd mrs caroline was dead and one of the
mis fillmores I tele him the was nothing of it you dident say
anything about it in your letter he sends his best love to her
and all the family he was verry uneaSy about misS caroline
he came over to our Redgmt to Se me to know if it was so the
is nothing but hard times down hear I saw in the papers this
morning that general jackson died yesterday at three oclock
tel nat not to disappoint me I will do as I said I kno the way
thomas Seay and little nienks went to the yankeys when we
left Suffolk the yankeys took about three hundred prisners
when the army fell back from Suffolk that is all I know
now giv my lov to mother and all the family and I send my
best lov to you in prefrence of all the Rest nothing more but
Remains your tru husband yours sencearly M B Thurman
to Mrs jane R Thurman 14th virginia Redgemt
armisteads Brigade Pickits Division*

81

We now come to the first letter from Merit's brother, Robert, to Jane. Responding to a letter from Jane, Robert sent her love from Grandison, Robert and Merit's other brother. (Both Robert and Grandison were in Company D, 41st Virginia Infantry which consisted principally of men from the Clover Hill coal mines located near Winterpock. The 41st Virginia kept excellent records of its men.) What follows are Robert and Grandison's service records:

Thurman, Grandison W.: enlisted June 15, 1861, Clover Hill District, Chesterfield County for one year; private Company D; illiterate; 5'7", gray eyes, dark brown hair; corporal summer 1861; reenlisted for war March 1862, received $50 bounty; reduced to private April 1862; on special duty May 1862, searching for deserters, Chesterfield County; on special duty January 1862–April 1863 with provost guard; POW Burgess's Mill October 27, 1864; at Point Lookout October 31, 1864–June 21, 1865.[18]

Thurman, Robert H.: enlisted June 15, 1861, Clover Hill District, Chesterfield County for one year; private Company D; corporal summer 1861; reenlisted for war March 1862, received $50 bounty; May 1862 on special duty searching for deserters; Wounded in Action Glendale June 30, 1862, gunshot, side; at Chimborazo Hospital No. 1, June–July 1862; home on sick furlough July–October 1862; at Chimborazo Hospital No. 4, October 1862, dysentery; detailed light duty, nurse, Chimborazo Hospital No. 4, October 28, 1862–March 1863; Killed in Action Crater July 30, 1864; became 1st sergeant, date unknown.[19]

Robert's regiment, the 41st Virginia, was in camp at Hamilton's Crossing—on the Richmond Fredericksburg and Potomac Railroad just south of Fredericksburg—when he penned the following letter.[20] Robert and the 41st Virginia in Mahone's Brigade marched and fought (in the Battle of Chancellorsville) for eight straight days, as he reported to Jane. A letter from her had arrived a few weeks earlier. One of his reasons for writing was his concern about his brother, Merit, from whom he had not heard for some time. (Note that Robert used Meredith's family nickname, "Merit," in the letter. Note also that Robert capitalized his "Bs" and "Rs" as did his brother Merit.)

The return address on the back of the letter is as follows:

Addrefs
R. H. Thurman
Co. D. 41st Va Regt
Mahone's Brigade
Andersons Division
Near Fredericks Burg Va

The letter is as follows:

Camp Near Fredericks Burg
May 18th 1863

Dear sister. With pleasure I write you a few lines in answer to your much welcomed letter I Received from you a few weeks ago I was glad to hear from you and hear you were well and I hope this may find you as well as it leaves me at this time I have seen a hard time since I heard from you I was marching and fighting for 8 days But thank god I never got hirt two of my company was slightly wounded Dear sister answer this as soon as you can and let me no when you heard from merit I am very ancious to hear from him I would have writen to you Before now But I never had the

chance to do so   I hope you will excuse me for it   Brother
Grandison sends his love to you and says he would be glad
to see you   it is nearly time for drill so I must come to a close
By saying I am ever your Devoted Brother.   R. H. Thurman
/ Written in a hurry
send my love to merit when you write to him   GoodBye

Merit's company left Falling Creek on May 15 and
marched to Hanover Junction, reaching that location two days
later. They remained until June 2, 1863.[21] The following letter
from Merit was the most depressing that he had written, thus far,
to his wife. Since the regiment's arrival at the rail junction, many
of the other soldier's wives had come to visit. Jane had not. Merit
was so upset that he imagined her, back home, enjoying someone
else's company. He had found her a decent place to stay should
she visit; he had even gone over to the junction six times, hoping
to see her step off a train. No Jane. (In her defense, it would have
been quite an undertaking for a seventeen-year-old woman to
travel by train, alone, in wartime—especially if she had never
been away from home before.)

may the 26th 1863

my dear wife   I seat my Self this morning to write a few
more lines to you to inform you I am well an in hopes when
these few lines coms they may find you well and injoying the
greatest of plesure   I am sorry that you disappointed me so
by not coming down to se me when I wrote for you   I know
you could of come if you would but I suppose you had Rather
injoy som boddy elses company them mine   I feel myself
almost forsaken   I never had my feelings hert so bad before
to think one that I think so much of and love so dearly

and esteem so highly then for you to treat me so I hav
forsakened every boddy in the world for you and is willing
to die for you I am coming up in a few days so you may look
for me untel you se me but I am fraid you don't want me to
come but I am coming onest more any how to se what is the
matter I herd from you twice since I hav bin to hanover
junction I hav bin to the junction six times to meat you
and I got a good place for you to board at but you did not
come evry boddys else wife came to se them and I know you
could come if you had wanted to come you hav no excuse
for not coming it is not worth while to write any more now
for I am going in a few days I know I hav not don anything
to hert your feelings if I did I did not know it I will now
bring my letter to a close in hopes to se you in a short time
Yours most sencearly
M B Thurman
14th Virginia Redgemt hanover junction armisteads
Brigade
Pickits division

Armistead's Brigade—including our letter-writer toting
a musket in the ranks of the 14th Virginia—left Hanover Court
House on June 8 heading north. Robert E. Lee had once again
decided to take the war into enemy territory, Pennsylvania being
the ultimate goal. By June 11 Merit's company had marched as
far as Culpeper Court House. From that location he wrote the
following letter to Jane in response to one of hers. He noted
that he had just written her a letter—which, unfortunately is
missing—and had "started it" before he received her "kind and
affectionate letter" and decided to write what appears below.
Merit wrote in this letter that she must write whether or not she
receives anything from him.

Evidently, the worries expressed in the missive of May 26 were completely misplaced as Jane must have arrived almost immediately thereafter to visit for a few days. (On June 3–6 the 14th Virginia had been busy going after Federal cavalry in Caroline, King and Queen, and King William Counties and returned to Hanover Court House on June 7.[22] They departed the next day, so the only time Merit and Jane could have had together was between May 26 and June 3.) Merit was glad she was pleased with her trip to Hanover Junction.

He expected to be marching everyday, but as long as he could find paper, pen, and ink, he would write. Merit was still hoping that Jane could get him out of the war. No doubt he was still thinking about an assignment to a government boat. He noted that "Mr. Flanagan" would know what to do. ("Mr. Flanagan," most likely, was the owner of Flanagan's Mill at Buck Island on the Rivanna River Canal.[23] According to one of Merit's letters, he and Jane had spent time there together. Flanagan's Mill was within two miles of Union Mills where they were married. The river port known as Flanagan's Landing featured a store and the Flanagan homesite. Flanagan's Mill and Flanagan's Landing may have been one-in-the-same, The Buck Island location for Mr. Flanagan is the most likely as it also had another mill nearby.) If Jane could get the "detail" for Merit, he would come.

At the end of his letter, Merit attached two more love poems to Jane. He was quite a poet.

Additionally, he told his wife not to visit his mother if she did not write. (This is a bit mysterious as Merit's mother had wanted desperately to see Jane. Knowing that his mother died three months later, one wonders if she was sick with a contagious disease.)

culpepper county June the 11th 1863

*my dear loving and affectionate wife I take my pen in hand
this morning To write to you I received a letter from you
last night I had just wrote a letter and started it To you but
I thought I would answer This kind and and affectionate
letter that you wrote to me which almost made me shed tears
to Receive such a good letter from my dear good wife that I
think so much of and lov so dearly i would giv anything in
this world if I could just could liv with you oh how happy
I would be if I just was there with you one that I lov so
dearly and tru my dear loving frend I havent any news to
write this morning. I wrote all the news I had to write to
you yesterday we are in culpepper yet near the court house
but we are expecting to march evry day you must write to
me evry week you must not weight for me. if you dont get
letters from me it is not becaus I dont write. I will write
to you as long is I liv and can get pen and ink and paper
becaus I know you is the best frend I hav in this world and
I lov you just as hard is I can lov you I cant lov you any
better Then I do lov you I am glad that you was so well
pleased with your trip to hanover junction but I dident treat
you half as well is I wanted to treat you I hope This wicked
war will end before long so is I can come home to liv with
you and liv as we ought to liv you do all you can for me but
I know you will and I will try and do the best I can untel
you get me off out of this war all I want is just to get there
to liv with you in peace and I will be Satisfied I wouldent
want any better heven if I just could get there to liv with my
dear good and pretty little wife that is all I want to comfort
me in this world I havent any more to write this time you
must write to me evry week you are all the pleasure for me*

in this world   you must write me word whether you got
the letters I wrote to you or no I will   if you get the detail
for me send it on to me and no matter where I am I will
come   mr flanagan will know what to do about it   I will
now bring my letter to a close by saing I yet Remains your
tru and affectionate husband untel death part us from this
unfrendly wicked world   Yours most Sencearly
M B Thurman
To Mrs jane R Thurman
14th Virginia Redgement   Company C
Amsteds Brigde Pickits Division
I loved you then I lov you still
I lov you now and allways will
So good by hopeing to Se you again
In a short time   you must pray for me
I might get killed yet
M B T
To Mrs j B T
The happyest hours I ever injoyed in
This world was when I was with
My dear pretty little girl
[in margin] dont go to se mother if She don't write for you.

Merit penned the following letter on June 12, the day
after his last one. His company remained near Culpeper Court
House—Lee's army was gathering there for the march north.
Rumors were afloat that they were headed toward Maryland
again or Pennsylvania. He was not sure if he should go with
them into the Northern states as he might not see Jane again. He
wrote that he would come home in August. Merit had reenlisted
and was supposed to receive either a thirty-six-day leave or
payment for that time period. "[I]f I get killed or die," he wrote,

"I want you hav evry thing that is coming to me." He noted that "montilea clarke"—meaning 1st Lieut. Montilla Clark—was the 14th Virginia's paymaster.[24]

Merit also reported, rather pessimistically, on the Battle of Brandy Station, fought on June 9, 1863. (The enemy had taken the offensive in this fight, and it was the first time the Yankee cavalry held its own. The total losses were 523 Confederates and 936 Federals.[25] The two colonels Merit mentioned are Frank Hampton and Calbraith Butler.[26] Merit was more accurate about the Stevensburg battle. In holding back a flanking Union cavalry force, the 4th Virginia Cavalry lost its horses as well as half of its men captured.[27])

Once again, after the end of his letter, Merit wrote a love poem to Jane.

culpepper court house June 12th 1863

My dear loving Wife I sent my Self this morning to write to you onest more to let you hear from me I am right well at this time and I truly hope when these few lines comes to hand they may find you injoying all the blessings this world can afford you I hav not received but one letter from you since I saw you but I know your letter has not had time to to get hear yet and I know you would not fail to write to me the army had to march again the next morning after I wrote to you last we are now in culpepper in three mile of the court house we are now in camp but I dont know how long we will stay hear they talk of going threw maryland again or pensylvania and if they do go I hardly know what to do about going with them if I go I might not never se you

*any more   I know if they do go they will hav a heep of hard
fighting to do but I will do what I think is for us both   you
must make your Self contented and do the best you can   I
hope and trust it will not be long before we can get together
so iS we can liv happy forever   I know the never will be
know more pleasure for me without you   I know I never
would find another one that I love so dearly aS I do you
and one that is so kind and affectionate to me as you are   I
know if any boddy ever did hav a good wife I hav got one
and a pretty one too and I cant help from loving you better
then everything in the world   if I just was there with you
now I would be happy   I just wrote a letter to your brother
pueinton yesterday and I thought I would write another
one to you to day   the yankeys took seven hundred negroes
and three hundred horses in King William county last week
and steward and the yankeys had a hard fight hard fight at
stevensburg three days a go in culpepper county   the yankeys
whiped our men badly   they killed three of our colnals and
five hundred horses and killed a great many more men but
they hav not asertained the number was killed yet   they
took one Redgement of our men prisners   the yankeys lost
som men too but nothing like as many as we lost on our side
the yankeys is in about eight mile of uS now   I dont know
what time we may get in to the fight   they are cross this Side
of the Raperhanock River now weighting for us to come   I
havent anymore to write this time   you must write to me
as often as you can   you must not weight for me and I will
not weight for you   I am coming home in august if I can   if
anything Should happen to me ther is one hundred and 25
dollarS due me for clothing money the first of november and
they promised to giv the souldiers 40 days firlow in a year
and if they dident giv it to them they said they would pay*

them the money for it and they hav never giv me the thirty
siz days firlow yet for Reinlisting they say they are going to
pay the men for the thirty six days if they dont giv the firlow
to them if I get killed or die I want you hav evry thing
that is coming to me and if I liv I intend for you to hav evry
thing I makes as long is I liv montilea clarke iS the man to
pay it to you he pays all the men in the 14th Redgmt you
are all that I liv for in this world and you are all that I lov
tel mr page not to think hard of me not writing to him I
will write to him before long giv my best lov and Respects
to him and his family and giv my best lov to your mother
and miss caroline and all your sisters and kiss all of them
for me I would be mighty glad to se them all and giv my
Respects to all inquiring frends I hav know more to write
this time of importance you must write to me as soon as you
can I will now bring my bad letter to a close by saing I still
Remains your affectionate loving husband and will Remain
so as long as life last   your sencearly
M B Thurman to Mrs jane R Thurman
My dear loving wife
the happyest times I ever sent in all my life was when I was
with my dear good little loving wife
the happyest hours I ever Se was when I had you along with me
our time is short our days are few the happyest hours I ever
spent was along with you
the good days we hav spent is past and gone and now the
hard times is coming on
but yet I hope all things will work out for the best
I married you for your buty and good qualitys and becaus
you was a good little girl and now lov you better and think
more of you then evrything in the world
we are now many many miles apart but yet I think of you

91

and lov you with all my soul and heart
fare you well my dear wife one who I love is I do my own
dear life   fare you well for a while
hopeing to se you in a short time again
direct your letters to M B Thurman
14th Virginia Redgement
Culpepper C. H.
Armisteds Brigade
Pickits division

When Merit wrote his letter of June 19, he had been on the march an entire week. Somehow he found the necessary materials, and the time during a short halt, to write his wife. He was very tired from marching as they had tramped from Culpeper County to somewhere in Fauquier Coounty during extremely hot weather. Six soldiers had died from heat exhaustion on the very first day of their march. Others had died along the way. He guessed correctly that Maryland was the army's immediate destination, but he did not know that General Lee planned to continue on into Pennsylvania.

(Jane's letters meant so much to him as they connected the two spouses. During the war, letters from home meant everything to the young soldiers—they kept them going. Merit mentioned that he had money to send her, but was afraid that the Yankees might intercept it. Yankee cavalry must have been nearby, occasionally harassing the march columns and supply trains.)

June the 19th 1863
fauquire county
Virginia

my dear loving wife   I Seat my Self to write a few lineS to
you to let you hear from me   I am well at this time but verry
tired marching I hope thiS may find you well and injoying
all the blessings god can afford you in this world I received a
letter from you the 16th of june but we was on a march and I
did not hav time to anSwer it but the army is made a little halt
now and I will write a few lines to you to let you know where
I am but I havent got time to write much I was mighty glad
to hear from you it makeS me feel Rejoyest to read your good
affectionate letters the is nothing in this world can afford me
as much pleasure without I could se you I dreamed about a
few nights ago I thought I had you in my armS hugging you
and I felt So glad I dident know what to do but when I waked
you want there what a joyful time it would be if I just live with
you the is none but you can make me happy in thiS world The
Soldiers is dying all along on the road by getting over heat the
was Six died the first day we Started from culpepper I havent
any more to write but I expect the army will go to maryland
but we will hav Som fighting to do first my dear Rosser you
must do the best you can and be a good girl untel I come back
the is nothing can Stop me from coming back to you without it
iS death. I lov you So dearly and think so much of you I will
never be happy without you I would Send you Som money in
this letter but I am fred to Send it the yankeys is all about hear
in the mountains I dont know is you will ever get thiS letter
They might get our mail I will now bring my letter to a close by
saying I still Remains your tru frend and husband untel death
then I hope we will meat in heaven   yours sencearly

M B T Mrs. j R T goodby
direct your letters to Richmond Virginia
14th Virginia Regemt armisteds Brigade Pickitts division

Merit wrote to Jane two days later on June 21, during a short halt, with the latest news from the march north. His location he noted as "lowden county" (meaning "Loudoun County" in northern Virginia). The Shenandoah River was too high to ford when they arrived, so they had to wait a day for the water to subside. Merit wrote that 132 men in Pickett's Division had died from the heat on the march. None had died in Company C, 14th Virginia Infantry, but some of the men were "verry bad off." Tell Mr. Westcoat, he asked Jane, that his son Jim was well. He missed Jane's letters—he had only received the one Jane and Ellen wrote him as he started the march north. He was still afraid to send money as the Yankees were "nearly all around us." Evidently, Yankee cavalry had been very active around Lee's moving army as Reuben Boston and his brother, Fontaine Boston, of the 5th Virginia Cavalry were captured along with most of their company.[28] James W. Allegree of the 5th Virginia Cavalry was also wounded and captured in the fight at Aldie, Virginia, on June 17. He was paroled the same day.[29] Allegree's horse was killed and he was paid $833.00 for it.[30] Merit believed they were going on a roundabout way to get to Maryland.

Lowden county Virginia
june the 21, 1863

my dear loving wife I take my pen in hand this morning to write a few lines To you to let you hear from me I am write well at this time and I hope when this reaches you it may find you well and injoying all the blesings god can afford you in this world I am now in lowden county we just crosS the Shanado River yesterday they all had to ford the river the water was So high when we got to the river we had to weight one day for it to fall it is bin Reigning verry hard hear for

*two days   we had Som very hard marching but I am not
hert yet   one hundred and thirty two men died in pickitts
division on this march from the heat   the weather is very
hot   the is none of the men in our company dead yet but
Som is verry bad off   tell Mr wescoat jim is well   we hav not
bin in any fight sence we hav bin on this march but I don't
know how Soon   the yankeys is before us and behind uS   we
can hear them fighting behind us evry day   I am in verry
good Spirits yet   I still liv in hopes to se my dear good wife
again the one I lov so dearly   my dear Rosser you must write
to me as soon as you can   I Received the letter you and Sister
Elen wrote to me the first day we started which I mintioned
in the other letter   I would send you Som money but I dont
know as you will ever get this letter   the yankeys is nearly all
around us   the yankeys is got Rhubin Boston and fountain
Boston and all the company but eleven of Them one man
killed and som few wounded   jim alegray was wounded
and taken prisner   I hav not time to write any more   The
army is going on in a little while   I think they are going in
the direction of maryland in a Round about way   my dear
make your self contented and do the best you can untel I
com back   I hope I can stay with you when I com back   I am
willing to die for you   I still Remains your tru loving and
affectionate husband untel death parts us   yours sencearly
from my hart   when we meat again I hope we will never
part   M B Thurman to Mrs J R T
direct your letter to culpeper C. H.   14th Va Regmt*

Merit penned this undated letter at the end of June after
his brigade arrived in Franklin County, Pennsylvania, just south
of Chambersburg. In a letter he had just received from Jane, she
told him that she did not want him to go north out of Virginia.

If he had known her wishes, he wrote in the following, he would
not have marched out of the Old Dominion. Merit promised
Jane that he was going to come to her after she sends for him.
(Merit missed Jane terribly and planned again to go AWOL.)

   Merit said that his brothers were also in Pennsylvania
although he had yet to see them. He told Jane to relay to Mrs.
Wescoat and Mrs. Harlow that their sons were well, so they must
have been with him in his company. He also sent his love to Jane's
family as well as to the family of Mr. Page.

the state of pensylvania
Franklin county

my dear affectionate loving wife I Seat my Self to write to
you onest more to let you hear from me tho it may be the
last opotunity but I am in hopes to liv to se you onest more
I Received your kind and affectionate letter this morning
and the is nothing in this world could afford me as much
pleasure as to hear from you and to hear you was well I
am Right well at this time and I hope to god when you
get this letter it may find you injoying all the blesings and
comfort in this world that god can afford you my dear
wife you must make your Self contented and do the best you
can untel I come back I am coming back if god spars me to
live to se old Virginia again I would not of come if I had
known you dident want me to come but I thought it was
for the best and I am in hopes yet it will turn out for the
best god knows I think more of you then evry boddy in this
world and the iS nothing cant part me from you without
it is death and if I never would se you anymore I would be
Ruined for ever it would be a death blow to me you must

do the best you can for me and when ever you Send for me
I will come   you must write to me as often as you can   I am
fred our mail line will be stoped   the Yankeys is scouting
about evry where   as soon as you get Ready for me write me
word and I will come no matter where I am   I dont know
how long the army will Stay in pensylvania   we havent had
any fight hear yet but we are expecting a big fight hear Soon
giv my best lov to mother and all the famly and mr page
and famly and brother perinton and famly also   Brother
Robert and Grandison is in pensylvania but I hav not Seen
them yet   tel mrs wescoat jim is well and tel mrs harlow jim
harlow is well too   no more for this time but I RemainS
your tru loving affectionate husband untel death parts us
from this unfrendly world
M B Thurman to mrs jane R Thurman my dear good loving
wife.

A lot had happened to the 14th Virginia since Merit's
last letter. On July 2, 1863, Pickett's Division—consisting of
Armistead's, Kemper's, and Garnett's Brigades—marched to
Gettysburg, Pennsylvania, arriving in the afternoon.[31] It was
the second day of the massive three-day Battle of Gettysburg.
On July 3 Lee planned to attack the Union center on Cemetery
Ridge as he felt it might be weak. (He had previously attacked
both of the Federal flanks and failed.) A low stone wall and a
copse of trees marked the attack's goal. Union Gen. George
Gordon Meade advised his generals that Lee might try his center
on July 3. Lee planned to attack with three divisions totaling
about 11,000 men. Pickett's Division of Longstreet's Corps—
including Armistead's Brigade with the 14th Virginia—would
send 5,800 men into the attack.[32]

97

The men of the 14th Virginia rose at 3:00 a.m. and
marched to their assembly area behind Seminary Ridge and
a long line of Confederate cannon.[33] General Longstreet had
serious doubts about the attack's possibilities for success because
the Southerners would have to cross a mile of open ground under
fire. Lee, however, overrode him.[34] As the pre-assault cannonade
ended, General Pickett said to his men, "Charge the enemy and
remember old Virginia!" General Armistead's oratory included,
"Remember! You are fighting for your liberties; strike for your
homes, your wives, and your sweethearts. Follow me!"[35]

In the attack Kemper's Brigade was on the right, Garnett's
on the left, and Armistead's behind the center ready to assist
either.[36] The enemy fire was overwhelming as the assault force
traversed the open ground. Canister rounds shivered their
ranks as they closed with the enemy. As they approached the
fence at the Emmittsburg Road, General Armistead put his hat
on his sword and led his men across. A hundred yards further,
Armistead crossed the rock wall at the union lines with about
150 of his men. He led his men toward an artillary piece and
was mortally wounded almost immediately[37]. When the enemy
forces converged, chaos reigned. The fighting was hand-to-hand.
Though the Confederates had penetrated the Union line, they
had lost so many men in the process that they could not hold on.
Union reserve forces appeared on all quarters. There was no other
solution—they had to run. Some later said it was worse retreating
than it had been attacking.

Of the 5,800 men of Pickett's Division who went
into the attack, only 1,000 answered roll call on July 4.[38] (It's
understandable, therefore, that Merit believed that only nine
men in his company survived Pickett's Charge.) The 14th

Virginia took 476 men into the attack and suffered 247 casualties for a total loss of 51.9 percent.[39] Merit's company—which listed fifty-six men—suffered thirty-two casualties for a total of 57.1 percent. All together, his company lost 75 percent of its officers and non-commissioned officers, and 52.3 percent of its privates.[40] Pickett's Division, in that one attack, lost most of its leadership.

Merit wrote his letter of July 9 while the army was waiting, in Maryland, for the Potomac River to be bridged. They evidently had 5,000 Yankee prisoners in tow and an enormous amount of loot. While there, Merit had received a letter from Jane saying she was unable to get him attached to a government boat. He answered Jane's letter with the following, including his report of Pickett's Charge. (His estimate of Pickett's Division losing one half of its men was not far off.) Merit noted that nearly all the officers in the 14th and 57th Virginia Regiments were killed (which was close to what the official records recorded). He then listed the company and regimental officers that he thought were killed. He probably saw some of these officers get wounded and thought they were killed, but he was right on a number of them. Merit reported that Jim Harlow (Company H, 57th Virginia), fell on the battlefield and was captured, but he did not know if he survived. [41] Merit's brothers survived the Battle of Gettysburg, along with cousin Beverly Ammonett who was in Company D of the 41st Virginia.[42]

He also mentioned Henry Harlow, Thomas Harlow, and Peter Harlow as coming out of the battle alive. (Henry and Thomas Harlow had been boatman at Union Mills before the war, and if "Peter" is a nickname for William Alonzo Harlow, he was a factory hand at Union Mills.[43] Peter could also have been a nickname for another brother, Alexander H. R. Harlow.[44] All four brothers were privates in Company F of the 44th Virginia Infantry.[45] Harris Jeniner may be Isaac Janney of Company A of the 57th Virginia.[46] "[C]olnal owen" was actually Major John C. Owens of the 9th Virginia who was wounded and died on July 4.[47] Colonel Edmonds was Colonel Edward C. Edmonds of the 38th Virginia who was killed in the attack.[48] Haden Martan was Sgt. Joseph Haden Martin in Company C. He was captured.[49])

Finally, at the end of the letter, Merit asked Jane to pray for him as he may not live long. Earlier in the letter he said he was coming to see her again if he lived long enough. (One can understand what he was feeling, especially after what he had been through in the attack on July 3. When Jane received this letter she probably wanted him to come home, furlough or no furlough.)

(I wish to add a personal note about my feelings when I retraced Pickett's Charge one summer day. I started at the jump-off spot near Lee's Statue and walked toward Cemetery Ridge at about what I felt was the attacker's speed. I was okay as I walked at a brisk pace to the Emmitsburg Road. As I crossed the fences and went the final hundred or so yards, however, I looked around and felt as if every cannon on the ridge was pointed at me. It was then that I realized the terrific fire the men had to charge through to get to the grove of trees. When I envisioned all those Union troops firing at Pickett's Division I broke down in tears. How the Southerners were slaughtered by the cannon- and rifle-fire.)

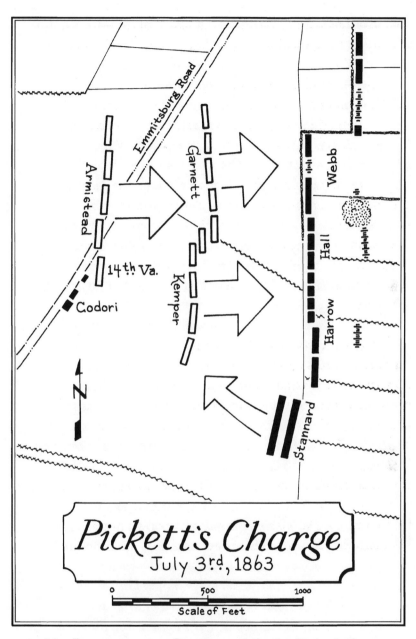

Map illustrating troop configurations at the battle of Pickett's Charge, near Gettysburg, PA. Map drawn by Rick Britton.

maryland
July 9ᵗʰ 1863

my dear Wife   I hav the pleasure of writing to you onest
more to let you hear from me   I am well at this time and
I hope when you Receive this it may find you well and
injoying all the blessings this world can afford you   I hav
bad news to tel you   we had a big fight in pensilvania and
more then half of pickets division was killed and wounded
the was seventy five of captain poores company went in the
fight and only nine came out Safte with my self   we are now
in maryland near the potomac River with five thousand
yankey prisners   I dont know how long we will stay hear nor
I dont know which way we will go from hear   I suppose the
prisners will be sent on to Richmond but I dont expect we
will go with them   I Received your letter yesterday and you
dont know how glad I was to hear from you   the is nothing
can afford me as much pleasure as to hear from you   I would
be glad to se you if I could   I am very sorry that you cant
get me off on the goverment boats   you said you thought I
had better not weight for that   I had better no what I was
talking about but if I do go I never expect to se you anymore
but I will do as you say about it but I had much Rather be
there on the River so is I could be with you   I had all most
Rather stay hear and be killed then to go away from you
So becaus I dont think you would ever come to me   I am
doing Right well at the present time but I am verry much
discontented in mine about you   I hardly know what to say
about it   I intend to Se you onest more if I can get to you if
I liv to Se that time   I all most as well be dead as to Se So
much trubble as I do about you   I lov you and think more
of you then evreything in the world but I cant Se no pleasure

*with you   it looks like evry thing works against me   you
are all that I lov in this world   I wish I had you hear with
me now   I am coming to se you onest more and if I liv long
enough and it will not be long   I hope I feel at a loss hear
now but if I was with you I would be all Right or had you
with me   all the officers in the 14th and 57th was killed
nearly and a great many privates   I will giv you the number
of them that I know is killed   colnal hogues was killed in the
14th   major was killed   Fill Seay   captain perkins killed
captain cogbill   captain logan and three more leutenants
colnal magruder and colnal Wade in the 57 was both killed
the yankeys took posesion of the battle ground   we did not
get our wound off   I cant begin to tel you all was killed   jim
harlow was seen to fall on the battle field   the yankeys is got
him   I dont know whether he is dead or no   brother Rober
and Granderson and bevly was in the fight but all came
out saft   henry harlow thomas and peter all came out Safte
harris jeniner came out saft   general armsted was mortally
wounded and taken prisner   general kemper was killed and
genral garnet was killed and colnal owen of the 9th Regemt
and colnal edmonds and so many privates I couldent tel   I
dont know them   haden martan is taken prisner or killed
I dont know which   we was three days fighting   the was a
great number of men killed on both Sides   the yankeys loss
was about 30 thousand and dont know what the number
was on our side lost   my dear wife you must write to me as
soon as you can and I will write to you again   I would be
glad to se you   I hav got Somthing for you   I havent any
more to write now but I still as ever Remains your tru and
loving husband untel death parts us from this unfrendly
world   I would write more but you know my mind is well
is I do my Self   giv my best lov to your mother and all the*

family   yours Sencearly
M B Thurman to Mrs jane R Thurman
My dear Wife
you must do the best you can and prey
for me   I may not liv long

The following letter was written from Bunker Hill, north of Winchester, Virginia. (Reading this letter, one can feel Merit's urgency—he desperately wanted to reunite with his wife. He ended this letter twice, the first time with another poem about death and his love for Jane.) Merit was very pessimistic about the South's chances of winning the war. In fact, he wrote that if Vicksburg had fallen as the papers reported, the South had already lost the contest. So many of Merit's friends and fellow soldiers had perished in Pennsylvania that he no longer wanted to be a part of the war effort. It was a lost cause.

His whole focus at this point was getting home to his wife. He wrote that as soon as he got close enough, he was coming. He thought they were escorting the Federal prisoners to Richmond, so perhaps he could leave from there. Merit went AWOL again on July 26, eleven days after he wrote the following letter. The 14th Virginia muster report for November to December, 1863, reported him as deserting from Culpeper Court House. Initially he was listed as AWOL, but when he did not return after a reasonable time, his status was changed to that of deserter. (It's not known whether he visited his mother in Richmond on his way home to Jane.) In the following Merit also told Jane to tell his "old friend to keep himself all write"— possibly a reference to Nat Bacon. This sad letter was the last Merit would write to his wife until the winter of 1864.

Bunkers Hill Virginia
July 15th 1863

*My dear loving good wife I seat my self to Write a few lines
to you this evening to let you hear from me I am well at
this time and I truly hope when these few lines coms to hand
they may find you injoying all the blessings and comfort
this world can afford you in this life. I Received a letter
from you last week and I had just written two letters to you
and we had to march then so I did not hav time to answer
it so I thought I would answer it now we are now in old
virginia onest more we are in Burkley county virginia 20
miles above winchester we are in camp to day but I dont
know how long we will stay hear but I think we will go on
towards winchester to morrow I am coming home as soon is
I can get near enough to come So you may look for me untel
you Se me I havent much to write to you this time Our
loss was great in pensilvania and maryland this time we
lost upwards of thirty thousand men and the yankey papers
says they lost thirty three thousand men killed wounded
and taken prisners we hav got one hundred yankey prisners
along with us now we may cary them on to Richmond but
I dont know yet if the division goes to Richmond I Recon I
will go to Richmond with them and then I will come home
from there I want to Se you worse then I ever did in my
life oh I hav seen so much trubble about you I began to
think that I never would Se my dear little wife any more but
thank god I am spard to liv this long and I am in hopes it
will not be long before I will Se you the one I lov So dearly
and tru I was sorry after I got to pensilvania that I ever
left Virginia but I am glad now I went as I came back safte
again I think this will be the last time I will ever go so fare*

105

*away from you again   if I ever go out of virginia any more
I will carry you with me   pensilvania and maryland is two
mighty good states to liv in and the is Som mighty good
people livs there   Som of them treated me mighty kind and
wanted me to Stay there and I would be treated well but I
could not bare the thoughts of being So fare away from you
I lived fine and got plenty to eat while I was there but I had
Rather be with you and eat bred alone then to be way from
you and hav all The kind treatment in the world becaus
the is no boddy in this world can make me happy but you
no matter how fare I go nor where I go   I hav the same lov
and warm feeling for you and nothing cant brake The lov I
hav for you without it is death   you are all I liv for in this
world   I will now bring my bad letter to a close by saying
I still as ever Remains your tru and loving husband and
will Remain so untel death parts us from This wicked and
unfrendly world
yours Sencearly
M. B. Thurman*

*I may yet be killed and on the
Battle field I may ly
But I will Think of you as long
as I liv and lov you untel I die*

*when I am dead and gone
and you are left alone
when This you Se   Think and Remember me*

*tel my old frend to keep him Self all write   the South cant
hold out much longer   vicksburg is taken so the papers says
Som Says it is not So but if it is So the South is bound to fall*

*I hav a heep to tel you when I Se you   I would giv any Thing
in this world to Se you and it Shall not be long before I will
Se you if I liv   evrything is at a loss hear   the is So many of
our men killed and gone   This is all I can write this time
you must write to me as soon as you can   I write to you untel
I come home as long is I can get pen ink and paper   nothing
more this time   good by for a while
Merit Branch Thurman
To my dear Wife Jane R Thurman
14th Virginia Redgement
armisteds Brigade
Pickitts division
look for me in three weeks if not sooner
look for me untel you Se me*

Chapter 4 Endnotes

1   Crews and Parrish, p. 150.
2   Ibid., p. 86.
3   Ibid., p. 124.
4   Hewitt, p. 354.
5   Kathleen R. Georg and John W. Busey, *Nothing But Glory; Pickett's Division at Gettysburg* (Hightstown, NJ, 1987), p. 469.
6   Crews and Parrish, p. 124.
7   Hewitt, p. 370.
8   Ibid.
9   Ibid., p. 355.
10 Ibid.
11 Georg and Busey, p. 458.
12 Crews and Parrish, p. 34.
13 Crews and Parrish, p. 117.
14 Georg and Busey, p. 468.
15 Ibid., p. 470 & 250.
16 Georg and Busby, p. 347.
17 Crews and Parrish, p. 139.
18 William D. Henderson, *41st Virginia Infantry* (Lynchburg, VA, 1986), p. 142.
19 Ibid.
20 Ibid., p. 42.
21 Hewitt, p. 370.
22 Hewitt, p. 170.
23 Trout and Runge, p. 12.
24 Crews and Parrish, p. 94.
25 Douglas Southall Freeman, *Lee's Lieutenants*, vol. III (New York, 1944), p. 13.
26 Ibid., p. 15.
27 Mark Mayo Boatner, *The Civil War Dictionary* (New York, 1959), p. 81.
28 Robert J. Driver Jr., *5th Virginia Cavalry* (Lynchburg, 1997), p. 186.

29   Ibid., p. 179

30   Ibid.

31   Crews and Parrish, p. 38.

32   Ibid.

33   Ibid.

34   Ibid.

35   Ibid., p. 39.

36   Ibid., p. 38.

37   Ibid., p. 42.

38   Wayne E. Motts, *Trust God and Fear Nothing* (Gettysburg, 1994), p. 46.

39   Georg and Busey, p. 507.

40   Ibid., p. 505.

41   Ibid., p. 469.

42   Henderson, p. 86.

43   Kevin C. Ruffner, *44th Virginia Infantry* (Lynchburg, 1987), p. 87.

44   Ibid.

45   Ibid.

46   Georg and Busey, p. 630.

47   Ibid., p. 389.

48   Ibid., p. 420.

49   Crews and Parrish, p. 120.

George Mills Thurman, Co. G, 12th North Carolina
Volunteers. Older brother of Merit Thurman.

Picture of Jane Rosser Humphries Thurman in later
life, possibly during her marriage to James H. Beach,
a miller.

William Decatur Thurman and his wife, Permelia Roberts Thurman. Older brother of Merit Thurman.

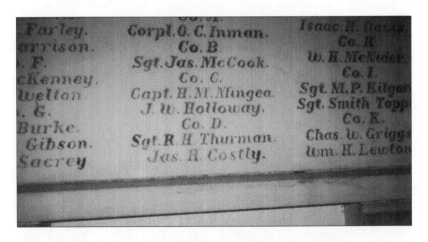

Plaque on the interior wall of Blandford Church at Petersburg with the name of Sgt. R.H. Thurman on it as one of Mahone's Brigade that was killed in action at the Battle of the Crater nearby and is in an unmarked grave in the church cemetery.

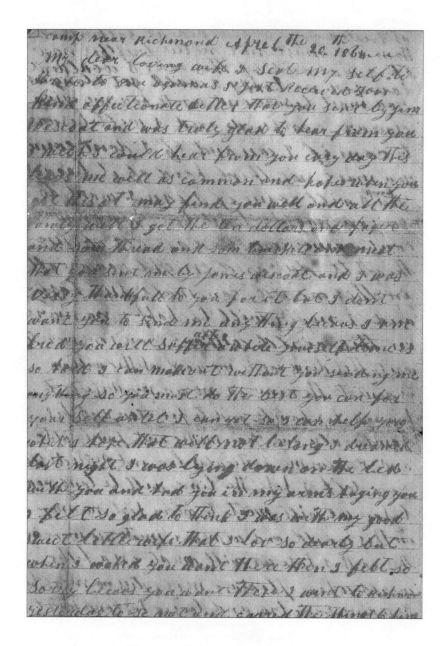

First page of a letter to Jane from Merit

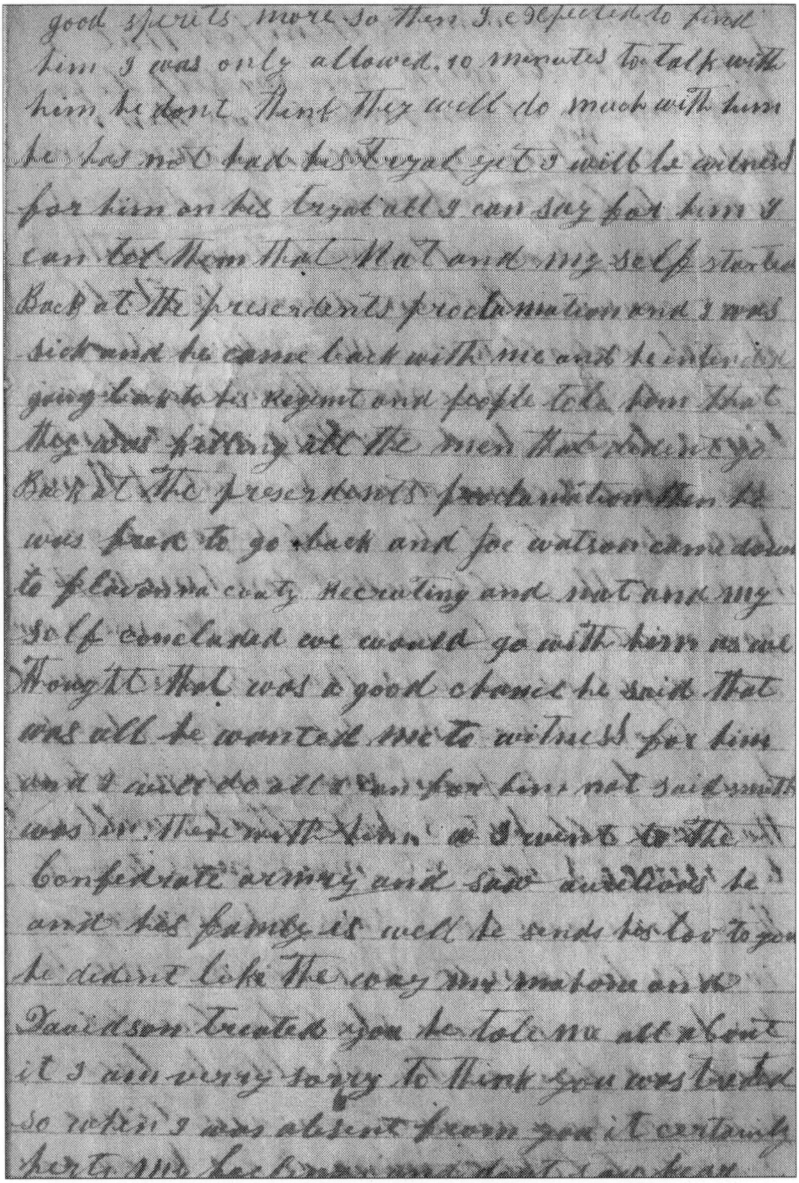

Page two of the same letter from Merit to Jane

Methodist-Episcopal Church , originally located in Union
Mills, where Merit and Jane were married on December
2, 1862. After the town of Union Mills died in the early
twentieth century, the church was moved to the north side of
Union Mills Road (Route 616).

Plaque on the church indicating that it was built in
1835 for the mill workers at Union Mills, which at
that time was located on the Rivanna River.

The only known original batteau remaining, located at Buchanan, Virginia, adjacent to the Community Center.

Batteau replicas of some of the boats that plied the James River and Kanawha Canal tied up at Cartersville during the annual Batteau Festival on their way from Lynchburg to Richmond.

One of the batteau replicas arriving at Cartersville during the annual Batteau Festival on its way from Lynchburg to Richmond on the James River. Note how the men poling the batteau walk back and forth on the planks on either side of the boat.

Jerusalem Baptist Church

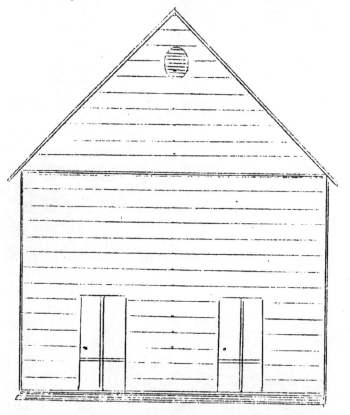

as remembered and sketched by the late
Mr. Beasley Hancock   c. 1910

Sunset Cemetery is in the major area where the
battle of Chester Station was fought.

Area in Sunset Cemetery where confederate soldiers killed in the
battle of Chester Station were buried in unmarked graves. The
Winfree House, where much of the action in the battle took place,
is in the background.

Chapter 5:
Death of the Soldier's Mother

This chapter covers an interlude—a lengthy gap in Merit's correspondence to Jane. As noted above, Merit had gone AWOL on July 26. He probably had no intention of ever going back to the army. (Presumably he was at home with his wife. Proof is in the following letter to Jane from Merit's brother, Robert, in which he said he was "glad to hear that Merit had goten home Saft." Merit and Jane were obviously together during September to perhaps early October, 1863, as Jane delivered her daughter, Anna Jane Thurman, on June 19, 1864. Perhaps, because Fluvanna County was so rural, Merit's presence was not noticed by the Home Guards, and perhaps he went into hiding whenever they drew near. Jane had probably nixed Merit's threat to fire back at them. At any rate, it seems Merit was home with Jane until at least the early part of 1864.)

What follows below are four letters from Merit's brother, Robert, and one from his brother, Aurelius. Their mother, Ann, was staying in Richmond with Aurelius and his wife, Nannie, at their home on Madison Street. (Nancy "Nannie" White

Thurman and Aurelius had married on December 23, 1862. Aurelius was a member of Company B, 1st Battalion, Virginia Infantry, Local Defense Troops. Aurelius was able to live at home most of the time.)

The following letter is from Robert to Jane, his sister-in-law. Robert had received a short letter from Jane telling him that his brother Merit was at home. Robert would have gone AWOL with Merit if he had not been sick at the time. Robert wrote that he did not want to experience another battle. Robert related the results of a "little battle" at Culpeper and mentioned a lightning strike that nearly fried two soldiers on the spot. One later died.

Robert had received a letter from his sweetheart in Clover Hill (where he had worked prior to the war). Evidently, his mother Ann was visiting her family. (Robert and Merit both capitalized the letter "R" when writing. And, strangely enough, Robert also capitalized "B" and "S" in nearly all of his words. Both brothers felt that their letters were badly written and often asked to be excused for their poor handwriting. Their families were very close and—as disease was so prevalent—they were always concerned about each other's health. They almost always wrote something akin to Robert's line in the following: "I was glad to hear from you and hear you were well.")

Orrange court House august 15th/63

Dear Sister I take the Pleasure to write a few lines in answer to your Short But much welcomed letter I Received yesterday I was glad to hear from you and hear you were well and also glad to hear that Merit had goten home Saft and hear he was well Sister I have Been unwell for nearly

*three weeks But I feel a little better today I truly hope this
may find you and all well I wish I could have gone with
Merit home But if I had of known when he was going I
could not have went with him as I was Sick at the time he
went But I will try to come and See you the first chance I
have we had a little fight at culpepeper on the first of this
month the 12th Va Redgiment had Six men wounded and
one captain killed we came here on the 4th of this month
and I cant Say whether we will have a fight here or not
But I hope if they do I may not Be in it for I never want
to go in another Battle and I intend to keep out if there is
any chance for it there was a bad accident here yesterday
Lightning Struck a tree and came very near killing two men
instantly one of them Died this morning and the other one
appears to Be a little Better and I hope he will get over it
they Belong to the 61st Va Regiment in Mahones Brigade
I they would move nearer Richmond So I could Run the
Block I am most too far from home to Run the Block as I
don't know any of the Road I Received a letter from clover
hill yesterday from my Sweet Heart She was quite well
mother is up there She was well and Sent her love to merit
give my love to Merit and if you get this Before you go to
Richmond give my love to aurelius and family and also
to mother if she is there which I hope She will Be give my
Respects to your mother I will come to a close please excuse
my Short and Badly writen letter I Remain as ever your
affectionate Brother
R. H. Thurman
To Mrs J H Thurman at home*

Ann Thurman returned to her home sometime after
Robert's letter of August 15 and was taken sick. She died on

September 10. Ann Thurman had been a devoted member of the Jerusalem Baptist Church.

The Jerusalem Church was a Baptist church that was formed June 12, 1852, when pastor David B. Winfree and twenty-two members were dismissed from Bethel Baptist Church for attending a barbeque. I attempted to find the foundations of the original church in the woods alongside present-day Route 60, but was unsuccessful. A service in memory of the Jerusalem Baptist Church was held on November 22, 1981. The information from the service leaflet is as follows:

WINFREE MEMORIAL BAPTIST CHURCH
1852–1981

Jerusalem Baptist Church, the forerunner of Winfree Memorial Baptist Church, was constituted with twenty-two members on June 12, 1852. The congregation and its pastor, the Rev. David B. Winfree, built its frame meeting-house on land given by member Higgason Hancock. The site, which included a cemetery, was about two miles east of the mother church, Bethel Baptist. An old minutes book dating from 1866–1881 lists 230 members. Feeling that the Midlothian Community needed more churches near the coal mines, the congregation hired in 1881 a contractor to roll the church to a new two-acre site, the present location. This land was given to the church by the coal mining Burroughs Estate. The church declined following the death of D. B. Winfree in 1888. Afternoon Sunday School was held in the 1890s under the leadership of Miss Loula Powell, local school teacher. The Rev. Robert

H. Winfree, son of D. B. Winfree, volunteered to preach
monthly. The ladies of the church helped raise funds
to build the present brick sanctuary in 1924. It was
renamed Winfree Memorial.[1]

The following obituary for Ann Thurman was published
in the Richmond Dispatch on September 17, 1863:

DIED

On the 10th of September, 1863, at the residence of
her son, on Madison street, after a short but painful
illiness of apoplexy, Mrs. ANN THURMAN, in her
67th year.

She was a strict member of Jerusalem Church,
and has been for many years. She leaves nine children
and many near and dear friends to mourn their
loss. She was a kind and devoted mother, and
beloved by all who knew her.
"Weep not for me, my friends and children dear,
I've gone to rest, you need not fear;
Our days on earth at best are but few,
Therefore prepare to follow me.

We bow in submission to His holy will;
Thy loss serves to bind us still closer to God;
The blow, though severe, still we will not deplore,
For soon we will meet thee where parting is no more."

Merit's brother, Robert, wrote the following—dated
September 15—after receiving a letter from Jane. He was at

Rapidan Station. It was a sad letter because Robert had just learned from his brother, Aurelius, that their mother was very ill. Robert tried to get a furlough to see her before she died, but it was refused. He hoped to meet her in heaven if he could not see her again in this world.

Robert also included a strong message for Jane and Merit: Do not "let them citizens take him up." Robert also mentioned the rumor that Pickett's Division had gone to Tennessee. Armistead's Brigade, however—what was left of it after Pickett's Charge—was still encamped near Petersburg. (Because of this Robert mentioned that Merit would not have to go to Tennessee—insinuating, perhaps, that Merit may want to rejoin his company. Robert was obviously very concerned about his brother, Merit.)

Orange County Sept 15th/63

My Dear Sister I take great pleasure in answering your kind and welcome letter that came to hand yesterday which found me well But I am in a great deal of trouble. I Received a letter from Brother Aurelius on the 13th stating that mother was very ill he Said she had Been SpeechleSs for two hours and Said if we ever wanted to See her again to come home as Soon as we could I Sent in an application for a furlough as Soon as I Received the letter But the news came that evening that the yankees were advancing and I think it will be very doubtfull about me geting home for we were ordered out the next morning to meet the enemy We are now near Rappadan Station Dear Sister, I have almost given up all hopes of ever Seeing my Dear Mother any more oh this war this war is an awfull thing But if I Should never

*see my Dear Mother again in this world I will try to meet
her in heaven oh this is a Sad time with me But I hope the
lord will Spar my Dear Mother for me to see her once more
But the lord noes Best what to do and I wish I could give
her up without grieveing after her But that is something I
can't do But I will live in hopes of Seeing her again in this
world But if I should not See her again I will try to meet her
in heaven Dear Sister I wish I could See you But god noes
when I will See you. Tell Merit not to let them citizens take
him up I heard that Pickett's Division was gone to East
Tennessee But I heard Armistead's Brigade was Camped
near Petersburg [Sentence not readable] Merit will not
have to go to Tennessee I havent Seen Brother Granderson
for a week But I will Send his love to you all cousin Beverly
Sends his love to you all give my love to all the family
and Receive a large Portion for yourSelf and Merit I will
conclude By Saying I am for ever your affectionate Brother
untell death good Bye
R. H. Thurman
This letter was written in a great hurry so I hope you will
look over all mistakes [Written upside down at top of second
page]*

In the following letter of September 28, 1863, Robert
answered a letter he had received from Jane the day before. As he
remarked sadly, his mother had passed away. Merit may not have
known about his mother's death, and perhaps had not traveled
to see her for fear of being caught. (From what Robert penned
about meeting his mother in heaven, it appears he was getting
serious about his faith in God.)

Based on this letter, Merit was obviously still at home with Jane in Fluvanna County. Robert asked her to relay to Merit his love and the recent news from the front lines.

Camp 41st Va Infantry
Orange county Sept 28th 1863

My Dear Sister I hasten to answer your Kind and welcome letter I Received yesterday the 27th I was glad to hear from you and of merit and hear that you all were well this leaves me in good health and I hope it finds you all enjoying the Same Blessing Sister you Said you were going down to See mother the 29th of this month But I am very Sorry to have to Say that my dear mother is dead She was taken Sick on the 10th of this month about 10 oclock in the morning and died that evening at half past six oclock I tried to get a furlough to go to her But I was Refussed So poor mother died and I never Saw her and will never See her again in this world I am going to her and meet her in heaven I have lost my Best friend in this world and I never expect to have another friend as good as my poor mother was to me She never Spoke But two words after She was taken Sick But I dont know what they were I wrote to Brother Aurelius to let me know what it was that She Said But I havent Received an answer from him yet I wish I new what mother Said Before She died we will never See her again But thank god there is a hope of meeting her in heaven She cant come to us But thank god we can go to her and if there is Such a thing as meeting in heaven I intend to meet her there where there will Be no more parting forever give my love to merit and tell him there is a plenty of yankees about here they are on the other Side of the Rappadan River

our pickett line is on the other Side of the Some times we get
a jankee Deserter over with us I dont think there will Be a
fight at this place But I Recon there will Be a fight Some where
about here Before very long we have all the advantage on our
Side of the River give my love to all the Family and Receive the
Same for yourself Grandison and Beverly Sends there love to
you all I will come to a close By Saying I Remain as ever your
affectionate Brother until death good Bye
R. H. Thurman
To Mrs Jane R Thurman
Write Soon [Upside down on second page]

Robert's previous letter—dated September 28,
1863—and the following letter from Aurelius on December 29,
represent the only extant correspondence to Jane during this
period from her brothers-in-law. (Either they were being cautious
or the other letters are missing. Maybe there was no need to write
with Merit still at home AWOL.)

The following changes in leadership took place during
Merit's absence. During the fall of 1863, Col. William White,
who miraculously survived Pickett's Charge with only a wound,
became commander of the 14th Virginia, and Gen. Seth Barton
succeeded Armistead as commander of the brigade (and thus
it became Barton's Brigade).[2] During the fall of 1863, Pickett's
Division—along with the 14th Virginia, Barton's Brigade—was
shifted back and forth between central Virginia and North
Carolina, finally spending December and January in Kinston,
North Carolina.[3]

Aurelius wrote to Jane expressing his regret at not
being able to get more than three days leave for a Christmas

visit. Because the leave was so short, Aurelius could not make it to Fluvanna County. He was concerned about Merit and asked her to tell him something about his brother in her next letter. Aurelius's wife, Nannie, had been very ill while visiting in Buckingham County, he wrote, but was well now. He and Nannie had moved to her sister's house on Duvall Street, in Richmond, and he asked Jane to come and visit. (Like his brothers, Aurelius capitalized "Rs," "Cs," and "Bs." Whoever taught the Thurman boys to write had a strange way of doing it.)

RiChmond
December the 29 1863

> *Dear sister   with much pleasure I take my pen in hand to write you a few lines to let you hear from us   this leaves myself and nanie well at present and hope these few lines may find you well also   I ReCeived your last letter in due time and was very glad to hear form you   I wrote a letter to you about too mounth Since and you had not Received it when you wrote your last letter   it was imposible for us to come to up there chris mass   I couldent get but three days absens from the army so at that Rate my visit wouldent have bin any pleasure for me   I wish you would let me hear some thing about merit when you write again   I have moved out on duvall street in part of the house with nanies Sister mrs. Robertson   you musent no wait for us to come   you must come when you can   nanie has bin up in BuCkinham about three weeks   I heard from her chrismass eve   she was very ill indeed   She Sent for davidson to come up as quickly as posible   I will close as havnt any more of importanC to write.   I Remain your devoted Brother*

> *Aurelius D. Thurman*

At the December 31, 1863, muster of the 14th Virginia, Merit's status was changed from AWOL to that of deserter (as he had been absent for over five months). If caught he was in serious, life-threatening trouble. (Perhaps by this period—February of 1864—he was living in the woods at times and was not able to see Jane as often.)

The final letter in this interlude was from Robert to Jane. Robert was concerned about Merit since Jane had not mentioned him in her last letter. (Merit's brothers, of course, wanted to hear from him.) Also, Robert thought he was getting a transfer to the Richmond city battalion—probably Aurelius's unit—but his colonel would not approve it. It was very cold, windy, and snowy along the Rapidan River where Robert's regiment was encamped.

Camp 41st Regt
February 17th 1864

Dear Sister Your kind letter of the 11 was gladly Received on the 13th and found me in good health and was also glad to hear that you were well.   This leaves me well and hope it may find you enjoying the Same BleSsing   there is no news of interest to write you   all is quiet on the Rappidan and I would be glad if it would Stay So   what have become of Merit   you dident Say any thing about him in your letter Sister I mentioned in my last letter of geting a transfer to the city Battalion   I did expect to get it But my Cornal will not approve of it   So I dont Reckon I will get it and I am Very Sorry I cant get the exchange   I am more dissatisfied than I have ever Been during this cruel war But I hope it will not last much longer   Sister I must Say I think you wrote your last letter with the Rong end of your pen   I wish I could

come and See you But I cant Say when I can come when I
went home on furlough I only had 15 days and you know
I wanted to See my Sweet heart therefore I had not the
time to go and See all that I wanted to See But I hope I may
Be Spared to See you Before too very long when ever you
write to merit Send him my love I would Be glad to See
him Brother Granderson is now working in the Brigade
Shoe Shop making Shoes for this Brigade he comes to See
me — nearly every day he is well and Sends his love to you
Beverly also they Send there love to merit and Says tell
merit to write to them give my love to all the Family and
Receive the Same for yourself it snowed here yesterday But
it is very clear and cold to day and the wind almost Blows
our tents down write often and write all the news I will
come to a close I am as ever your
affectionate Brother
R. H. Thurman

Chapter 5 Endnotes

1   Author Unknown, "Jerusalem Baptist Church," (Winfree Memorial Baptist Church, 1981).
2   Crews and Parrish, p. 46.
3   Ibid., p. 46–47.

Chapter 6:

A Soldier Returns to the Army

Merit wrote the following letter from Warm Springs, Virginia—in Bath County—after leaving Fluvanna. A "Mr. Watson," an army recruiter according to Merit in a later letter, had sent him to Warm Springs probably along with Nat and Jim Carver. (The Bath County springs were used as hospital sites during the Civil War, but there was no indication that Merit was hurt or ill, other than him using "right well" instead of "well" as he usually did in his letters). He was evidently attempting to join the cavalry. (He had advised others to join as they could ride instead of walk—a huge advantage considering the shortage of shoes in the Confederate Army.) The cavalry unit in question was Jackson's Brigade commanded by Col. William Lowther Jackson. A cousin of "Stonewall" who had served in the war since 1861, Jackson had just been given the brigade and was organizing it at Warm Springs.[1]

Since Merit was officially a deserter since the last 14th Virginia muster on December 31, 1863, he was using his first two names—"Meredith Branch"—in order to enlist. He asked

Jane to give her letters to Miss Pinkey King so she could "Send it in her letter." (Perhaps Miss King had a fiancé or husband in the same cavalry unit. There was an ambulance driver from Palmyra in Company C, 14th Virginia named Elias W. King who was possibly transporting 14th Virginia men to the hospitals near Warm Springs.[2])

Febuary the 18th 1864

*Dear wife I write you a few lines to let you hear form
me I hav landed Saft to my jurnys end we got to worm
springs to day Mr. watson Sent us on to the worm springs
to stay a while So aS we could be Saft I am right well and
I hope when these few lines comes to hand they may find
you well also and injoying all the bleSSins and comfort this
can afford you I havent time to write any more now it
is geting late in the night we hav just got hear you must
write as Soon as you can and I will not weight for you I
write again in a few days when you write direct your letters
to meredith Branch walkers batalion company A that is
my name now and giv your letters to miss pinkey King and
let her Send it in her letter nothing more but yet Remains
your tru husband untel death parts us
M B Thurman
To MrS Jane R Thurman
giv my best lov to your mother and all the family I will
write you a good letter the next time Be Sure and and
don't forget to direct your letters as I tell you direct them
to meredith Branch millburer Depot walkers bytalion
company A
M B Thurman*

Merit's next letter—dated February 21, 1864—included the first indication that he was not well. In it, he noted that he was "in hopes of being all write after a while." He revealed that he was "a few mile above the worm Springs," so he was not receiving treatment at the springs themselves. He wrote of promises he had made to Jane (which he may have made at their wedding). A Mr. King must have been with him as he asked Jane to insert her letter in Mr. King's. He was still using his first two names, but he signed the following with his real name.

February the 21. 1864

My dear RosSer   I onest more Seat my Self to write to you to let you hear from me   I am right well and hearty and I hope when this comes to hand it may find you well in health and injoying all the good blessings and comfort that god can afford you in this life   I would be mighty to Se you if it was So I could but I know I cant Se you now   So I will do the best I can untel I can Se you and you must do the Same and make your Self contented   I am in hopes I will be all write after a while   I am a few mile above the worm Springs and expects To stay about two or three weeks   I dont know when I can Send for you   we are way off in the mountains about twenty mile from the Railroad   So you know it wouldent soot to Send for you to come hear but I hope we will be at a better place before verry long   I havent any newS to write of any importance   I hope you will git thiS and answer it as Soon is you can   I want to hear from you mighty bad indeed   if I don't Send for you you must not think hard of it becaus you know I will do all I can for you   I never expect to Se old fluvanna anymore untel the war endS but I intend to comply with all the promiSeS I made to you or die trying

that iS all I can Say or do   the iS know uSe of writing
anymore now   giv my best lov and respects to all the family
I would write Some particUlarS to you but you know as
well iS I do   write as Soon iS you get this   nothing more
but Remains your tru and affectionate husband untel death
parts uS from this unfrendly world   So good by for a while
M   B   Thurman to Mrs J R T
when you write be sure and write like I tole you and put it
in mr kings letter
direct your letter to millburer Station
WalkerS bytalion Company A
jackSonS Brigade   JoneSeS division
north weston Virginia calvery
Bath county VA

In the following correspondence, Merit's brother, Robert,
answered a letter from Jane saying that Merit was okay. Robert
had been very concerned about his brother and asked Jane
to tell Merit to write him. In one sentence (which is partially
unreadable), Robert mentioned being on picket duty on the
Rapidan River for five days. (The town's name in this sentence
reads "_____kettsville." Unfortunately, there was no town near
the Rapidan whose name ended in "kettsville," so perhaps a
mistake was made in the transcription.)

Robert wrote that his regiment had been marching
back and forth between Gordonsville and Louisa Court House.
Also, he was concerned that the Yankees planned an advance
on Richmond via Petersburg. His location, Madison Station in
Orange County, was a healthy one—healthier, he felt, than along
the James below Richmond—and he did not want to go there.
Robert also said that he had heard from Grandison's family.

(Grandison was married to Mariah Elliott, a widow, and this was
the first time this branch of the Thurman family was mentioned in
these letters. Grandison's first wife, Ann Brown, had died.) Robert
also mentioned that some deserters had "come here or near here
last Sunday" who had been living in a cave. Which side they were
on, or what became of them, unfortunately, he did not say.

Camp Near Madison Station
41st Va Infantry
March 9th 1864

Dear Sister
with pleasure I hasten to answer your kind and
welcome letter which came to hand in due time I am
always glad to hear from you and hear you are well this
finds me well and truly hope it may find you enjoying the
Same blessings I was glad to hear from Merit and hear he
was well I wish I could See him But god noes when we will
meat again if we ever do But I hope we may Be Spared to
meat again I wish this cruel war would end and let us all
go home Some times I think it will never end in my time I
was on pickett the time the yankeys made the
_____kettsville we had to Stay on pickett five days on
the Rappidan River as all of this Brigade or Reather 4
Regiments Brigade went near to charlottesville But did
not Stay But a Short time we all came to our old camp
about 10 oclock in the night and had to march the next
morning at three oclock we went to gordonsville and
Stayed near there until late in the evening we were ordered
to Richmond we took the cars and went as far as louisa
court House we were then ordered Back to our camp where
we are now in camp I Supose the yankees came verry near

geting Richmond   it is thought that the yankees are fixing
to come up on the South Side of the James River By the
way of PetersBurg   if this is true I Reckon we will have to
go down there But I would Reather Stay up here   this is a
healthy place for Soldiers more So than it is down there   I
wish I could See you   I could talk with you   I wish Better
than I can write and I hope it will not Be long Before I will
have the pleasure of Seeing you   have you had a letter from
aurelius lately   when you write to Merit Send him my Best
love and tell him to write to me Soon   give my Respects to
all the family   Beverly and Grandison Sends there love to
you and Merit   I heard from Grandisons family a few days
ago   they were all well   there was Some deserters come here
or near here last Sunday   they were in a cave about five
miles from here   well I will close this uninteresting letter By
Saying I am as ever your affectionate Brother until death
R H Thurman
Co. D 41st Va Regt.
Mahones Brigade
Andersons Division
army of Northern Va

Merit, according to the following letter of March 29, had voluntarily returned to his company in the 14th Virginia. Colonel White called him a good soldier—because he had returned—and did not confine him to the guardhouse or Castle Thunder in Richmond. Lieutenant Frith was speaking up for Merit, as were his friends in the company, and his desertion charge had been lessened to "absence without leaf."[3] He would still have to stand trial, however. From what Merit wrote, Nat and Jim Carver, a private in Company C, had probably also been recruited with him and sent to Bath County.[4] Their trials were also coming up. Merit wished he had returned earlier and noted that it was better for him to remain. He had gotten his blanket coat and other things, so he was warm, but Merit worried about Jane walking in the deep snow. He hoped to send for her in about a month and said he would write often.

Direct your letter to the car of leutenant phrith
Co C
Camp near Richmond March 29th 1864.

To Mrs Jane R Thurman
My dear RoSSer   I take my pen in hand to write a few more
lines to you to let you hear from me aS I know you want to
hear how I am geting along so I will not Weight for you   I
will write evrytime I hav anything to write untel I get strate
I am Right well at this time and I Truly hope when you get
this it may find you well and injoying all the blessings and
comfort this world can Afford   I would be glad to be with
you now but the way Times iS now it iS best for me to be
hear for the iS but verry little pleaSure To be Seen at hom
now   you must do the best you can untel I se you again   I
hope it will not be long before we will meat to never part
know more in thiS world untel death parts uS   I am now
at the (word undistinguishable) doing Duty as same is
ever   colnal white wouldent put me in the gard house nor
cassle thunder   he Sid aS I had bin a good Souldier and
conducted my Self well before he would not be hard with me
but he Says I will hav to Stand a tryal   I am not charged
with desersion   I am only charged with absence without
leaf   leutenant Phrith Spoke up for me and do all he could
for me and So did all the men in the company   I would
bin charged with desersion if I had bin brought back but

as I Returned Volentearly I am only charged with absence without leaf jim carver is gone to Richmond to day to hav his tryal but I dont know what they will do with him yet nat is in cassle Thunder yet   I dont know when hiS tryal will come on   I would go there to se him but they will not let me. I got my blanket coat and all my things   I have know more news of importance   You must make your Self contented and don't truble your self know more then you can help for the is nothing but trubble now and so we hav to do the best we can   I liv in hopes to get out of thiS after a while   I wish I never had stade at home as long as I did   I would bin better off if I had stade hear   you must write me word how you are getting along and write me all the news   I will draw all my money that iS oweing to me   after a while I will Send for you to com to Richmond in about a month if the Regemt Stays Round Richmond.   I havent anymore to write So you must make your Self contented and do the best you can and think of me   I think more of you now then I ever did before   I am fred you will be Sick by walking in that deep snow   it makes me feel Sorry evry time I think about it   I lov you better then I ever did   I will die for you nothing more But Remains your tru husband untel death yours sencearly   M. B. Thurman To Mrs Jane Thurman 14th Va Regemt Bartons Brig Picketts division Longstreets Corp
care of leutenant phrith

Merit's next letter was penned April 7. A fellow private who had just returned to Company C—Jack Thomas from Fluvanna County—had seen Jane and said that she was well.[5] Private Thomas also told Merit that "haven and bony" had given themselves up. (These must have been nicknames for Fluvanna

County men in the company. At this stage of the war, with the Confederate ranks so depleted, it must have been very difficult for deserters and those "absent without leave" to continue evading the Home Guards and army details looking for them. Civilians were probably encouraging these men to return to the army voluntarily. The fact that Merit, Nathaniel Bacon, and Jim Carver—all of whom had been AWOL—were recruited and sent to Walker's Battalion at Warm Springs seems to support this.) The 14th Virginia at this time was stationed near Richmond to protect the city from enemy raiding parties.[6]

Merit also reported that Jim Carver had been tried, but had not been sentenced. (Carver was on a list of prisoners pardoned by President Jefferson Davis for volunteering to defend Richmond during Maj. Gen. Philip Sheridan's 1864 raid.[7] Sheridan's raid took place May 9–24, 1864, so Carver must have been kept in prison until then.[8]) Merit noted that a Mr. Sammand, who may have been a Fluvanna County resident, testified on Carver's behalf.

Nathaniel Bacon had his trial put off, but, according to Merit, Captain Rogers was "doing all he could against Nat." Bibby Vier from the 57th Virginia visited the 14th Virginia, however, and announced that, "leutenant Thomson Said he would do all he could for him." (There were two similarly named men in Nat's Company H of the 57th: Lieut. William Thomson and Lieut. Thomas W. Thompson.[9]) Nat was obviously in real trouble.

Finally, Merit told Jane that two men were "Branded on there behind with hot iron today for deserting and steeling out of the Regemt." (This information probably worried Jane—Merit

139

would have been wise to leave it out. If Merit's offense had not been downgraded from desertion to "absent without leave," branding could have been his punishment. Stealing was evidently punished pretty severely, especially when the perpetrator was also a deserter.)

Merit was very desirous of having "Perenton and Bill page" write to him. (A letter from home was tremendously important to a soldier in the field. One of their only connections to their friends and loved ones, it was a lifeline, so to speak, to their previous peacetime existence.)

Camp near Richmond april the 7th 1864

My dear affectionate wife   I Seat my Self this Morning to answer your kind and affectionate letter which I Received the fourth of the Present month and was truly glad to hear from you   I am well at this time and truly hope when you get this it may find you well and injoying all the blessings and comfort this world can afford   jack Thomas got hear last night   he Said he Saw you and you was well   I was glad to hear that you was well   he Said haven and bony had gave them Selves up and he gave me all the news   I havent had news to write this time mu Self evry thing is quiet----
------------present But we are expecting A big fight around Richmond now verry Soon   times is verry hard hear but I can make out as well iS the Rest   I am yet in the company as Same is ever   the other men I mentioned in my other letter is in cassle Thunder yet   they will hav there tryal today   jim carver has had his tryal but Sentance is not Read out yet he is at the company   when jim caver was at Richmond to his tryal nat was there too   nat he had his tryal put off   Mr

carver Said he had mr Sammand witneSs for him   Bibby
Vier was hear from the 57th Regmt Sunday last and said
captain Rogers waS doing all he could against nat and Said
leutenant Thomson Said he would do all he could for him
I dont beleav I hav anymore ness to write   yeS I hav too   the
was two men Branded on there behind with hot iron today
for deserting and steeling out of the Regemt Steeling cothes
that is all   I beleav you must do the best you can   I am
in hopeS the time will not be long before I can be with you
for you are all the pleasure for me in this world   The is no
pleasure for me without my dear little wife but I am doing
the best I can   I am living in hopes to go ------------- I am
doing now before verry long   that iS all for this time   giv
my lov to your mother and all the family   I would be glad
to Se all of Them   I will now bring my bad letter to a close
by Saying I still and will Remain your tru and affectionate
husband as long is life last   tel Perenton and Bill page they
must write to me   nothing more
yours most Sencearly M. B. Thurman
14th Virginia Regemt Bartons Brigade camp near Richmond
Picketts division in care of leutenant prith co C

The following letter from Merit was written in April of 1864. Jane had mentioned in a letter that she would like to come to Richmond to see Merit. For various good reasons, however, he was unsure whether she should come. Jack Thomas, who had recently returned from Fluvanna County, told Merit that Jane was considering traveling to Richmond with sister Ellen to see Nat, her husband. Merit penned that if she did, he would also go to Richmond as he expected to be at Nat's trial anyway. Jane and Ellen could stay at brother Aurelius's home while they were there. Just in case, Merit described the 14th Virginia's location. (The first part of this letter is missing and thus it is undated. It was probably written between Merit's letters of April 7 and April 11 because of the content, especially the mention of Jack Thomas.)

> you Said in your letter that you would like to com down To Richmond and Se me   if times was not So hard I would be glad for you to com but I dont know whether you could Se me or not   it wouldent Soot for you to come down to the camp   it is not a fit place for a lady to com   it is so muddy and bad and then they are expecting the yankeys to make an attack on uS all the time and they might cut the Railroad of so you could not get back   they wouldent hert you but I don't want them to get you   yet you know I would Rather Se you Then evry boddy else in the world   Nannie and Aurelious and all would be glad to Se you and would treat you well and if you want to come you come but then I am fred you might hav Som differculty and I know that wouldent Soot you   if we Stay Round Richmond and hav good luck I will Send for you in about two or three weeks Jack Thomas said you was talking about coming with Sister Ellen down to Se nat and if you do com with her I will try and com to Richmond if I know what day you come down   I will be at nats Tryal when his tryal comes on   if you Should com down the 14th Regemt is about 7 mile down the york River Railroad about a half a mile from the Railroad between the Railroad and Turn pike williamsburg Turnpike   I don't Beleav I hav any more To write so good by for thiS Time   you must write aS Soon aS you can   giv my Respects to all inquiring Frends
> Yours Sencearly
> M B Thurman
> 14th Virginia Regmt co C

Bartons Brigade
Pickitts Division

In the following letter of April 11—with its extremely long first sentence—Merit wrote that he was glad Jane and Ellen were able to visit Nat in Castle Thunder though he regretted not seeing his wife. Merit was having trouble getting a "permit" to visit his brother-in-law in that infamous prison warehouse. Merit had asked Jim Westcoat to call on Jane when he was home on a four-day furlough. Jim had "witnessed" for Merit at his trial and had offered to do so again. Merit wrote that his sister, Mariah, was being treated badly by her husband, Reuben P. Davidson, and that he was ashamed for Jane to know about it. Merit was so upset that he threatened to take Davidson's life. (Davidson was Mariah's second husband—her first, John L. Kiper, died in 1854 after only five years of marriage.)

In the following, Merit talked for the first time about the baby he and Jane were expecting. (The child would be named Anna Jane. She was my great-grandmother.) After what he had been through, Merit would probably not come home this time without a furlough. He told Jane not to send him any money as he could make out okay. Instead, he promised to send Jane money when he got some. Merit ended this letter with another of his poems about Jane.

Camp near Richmond april the 11th 1864

My dear Rosser I Seat my Self to write to you onest more to answer your kind letter which I Received a few minutes ago and was glad to hear from you and to hear you was well but was verry Sorry to think you was So close by me

143

and I dident se you but I Recon it was best becaus I know it would hert my feelings if I had Seen you and couldent Stade with you none and the wether is bin So bad you couldent injoyed your Self with me any hardly but I am glad you com down to Se nat   I hav bin trying to get a permit to go to Richmond to Se him my Self but I could not get it.   But I expect to go to Richmond in a few days to be tryed mySelf and I will Try and Se him if they let me in cassle Thunder to Se him   I havent much news to write   jim wescoat iS gone up home on a four days permit   I tole him to call and Se you and he Said he would So he can tel you how I am getting along   I had jim Summands for witneSS for me on my Tryal ------------to me when I got back to the Regemt [he] tole me to hav him summands and [he] would do all he could for me   [It is] not worth while talking about mr Davidson for he iS not worth talking about before he Shall treat my Sister as he has treated sister mariah and then go on So   I would take hiS life   I would Said Something to him about it when I came through Richmond but I was in one dificulty and I thought I would get out of that first   I would written to you about it but I was ashamed for you to know that my Sister had Such a mean low life husband   you must do the best you can untel I can Se you again and when you hav your little Baby you must be sure and write for me to come and if the iS any way in the world for me to come I will come for you iS all I hav to lov and care for in this world   it would be the greatest pleasure in this world for me if I just could stay with you but I know I cant so I must do the best I can and liv in hopes for better times which I am in hopes will not be long [becaus] the iS know boddy that ever [that I] thought know more of there [wife] then I do of you   I dont know iS [I ever] will com

back to fluvanna anymore [I dont] think I will without a
ferlow and whenever I Se where I can do better and hav a
good opotunity I intend to make good use of it and So you
must make your self contented the best you can about that
for no matter where I go or where I am carred to I will com
back to you or die Trying and you know I will I think evry
thing will work write before verry long I beleave all will
be brought to justice I havent anymore news for this time
So goodby and my god blesS you forever giv my Best lov
to your mother and all the famly and all the famly and tel
your mother I would be glad to Se her I will now bring my
letter to a close by Saying I Remains your tru husband and
frend untel death parts us from this unfrendly world jours
Sencearly
M B Thurman
14th Virginia Regemt co. C
BartonS Brigade
Pickitts Division
you said in your letter to let [you] know if I wanted any
money [Times] is hard hear but I can make -------- you
keep your money your Self [If I] hav luck I will be able to
send you money before long times iS Right hard hear but
I can make out verry Well at the present nothing more for
this time you must write aS Soon iS you can So good by
for thiS time
Merit B Thurman
To MrS Jane R Thurman

when thiS you Se Remember me
though many miles apart we be
our days on earth are few the happyest
times I ever spent was along with you

145

the happyest hours I ever spent in all
life was when I was along with & with my little wife

The next letter—dated April 12, 1864—was from Robert
to Jane. She had written him about Merit's visit and how she
hated to see him go back to the army. She did not know if she
would ever see him again. Robert wrote that they must put their
trust in God and if they did not see their friends again in this
life, they "aught to try and meet together in heaven where there
is no wars to part us." He hoped to see both his mother and Jane
in heaven. (Robert had evidently grown in his relationship with
God and one senses that he was trying to prepare Jane for his
and Merit's possible deaths on the battlefield. Robert claimed
that Merit used to be "mity wicked," but from Merit's letters we
see no evidence of anything but love for Jane and his desire to
be with her and help her. One wonders if Jane had some sort
of premonition of never seeing her husband again.) If Robert
survived the war, he planned to get a companion as he did not
like being alone.

Robert's company would be moving shortly as their
baggage had been sent to the rear. He said, however, that the
roads were so bad that they would not move for a few days. In the
spring of 1864 the Army of Northern Virginia would have to face
a new Union commander—Gen. U. S. Grant.

April 12th 1864
Dear Sister,
        I take this pleasant opportunity of writeing you
a few lines in answer to your kind and welcome letter of the
4th of the present month which came to hand a few days ago
and found me quite well   this also leaves me well and hope

when this comes to hand it may find you enjoying the Same
Blesfsing I am always glad to hear from you and merit
and hear you are well I am glad merit had the privilidge
of coming home for I know it was a few happy days with
him to Be with his family I Said I new it was a few happy
days with him But I dont have it But I think it would Be
with me and I believe it was with him But as for myself I
am one a lone But I think if I live to See this crull war end
I will try & have me a companion for I Believe I would Be
much happier than I am we are expecting to move every
day we have Sent all the Bagage to the Rear But the Roads
is So Bad I dont think we will move in Several days yet
You said you was Very Sorry to See merit Start Back to his
company I Reckon you was But you Said you dident know
as you would ever See him again that there was ten chances
— against him yes there is a thousand chances against him
and all of us But we must put our trust in god and not in
the things of this world and if it Should So happen that we
never more Shall meet with our near a dear friends in this
world we aught to try and meet together in heaven where
there is no wars to part us merit used to Be mity wicked
But I hope he is not So now we all aught to know that we
have got to die and we aught to prepar to meet god in peace
I hope to meet my dear mother there and I hope to meet you
there and I hope we all may meet together there where we
will Be happy forever I will close I Remain as ever your
devoted Brother R H Thurman
[upside down at top of second page of letter]
Granderson and Beverly Sends there Best love to you when
you write to merit Send our love to him and tell him to
write to us good Bye
Write soon

147

In the following Merit reported that he had received the things Jane sent him via Jim Westcoat (who had returned from leave). Merit told Jane, however, not to send him anything else "becaus I am fred you will Suffer after a while yourSelf." Merit had finally been able to see Nat, probably in Castle Thunder, and deliver items sent by Ellen. Even though he was going to testify on Nat's behalf Merit was allowed only a ten-minute visit. President Jefferson Davis had promised amnesty for those who were AWOL from the army if they returned. The others were expected to be executed. Merit planned to testify that Nat had been afraid to go back to his unit, so when Joe Watson came to Fluvanna to recruit them they decided to go with him as they felt it was their best chance for survival. Nat told Merit that Smith was in prison with him.

Merit also got to see Aurelius who did not like the way Jane had been treated by Davidson and Mr. Mahone. Merit referred to these men as lowlife characters. Jane wanted to know about the difficulty in which he was involved and if it had to do with Tump Smith. Merit noted that he had taken care of that situation and his fellow soldiers thought he had "don him right." (It is unclear which "Smith" Merit was referring to as there were several in his regiment.) Merit asked Jane to write him when she was confined and said that he would try to come home. (During this time, women stayed inside when they started to show as a result of their pregnancy, thus the word, "confined.") Merit referred to William and asked if he had gone into the army. ("William" was probably William Page—married to Jane's sister, Irene—who had been a witness at Merit and Jane's wedding.) Merit concluded by sending his respects to both William and Perrington, as well as to their families. Jane's brother Perrington must have been married by this time.

Camp near Richmond   April the 20th, 1864

*My dear loving wife   I Seat my Self to write to you again
as I just Received your kind affectionate letter that you
Sent by jim Wescoat and was truly glad to hear from you   I
wish I could hear from you evry day   This leavs me well as
common and hopes when you get this it may find you well
and all the family well   I got the ten dollars and paper and
som thread and som briskets and meat that you Sent me by
james wescoat and I was verry thankfull to you for it but I
dont want you to Send me any thing becaus I am fred you
will Suffer after a while yourSelf Times is So hard   I can
make out without you sending me anything So you must
do the best you can for your Self untel I can get So I can
help you which I hope that will not be long   I dreamed
last night I was lying down on the bed with you and I had
you in my arms huging you   I felt So glad ato think I was
with my good sweet little wife that I lov So dearly but when
I waked you want there   then I felt So Sorry becaus you
want there   I went to Richmond yesterday to Se nat and
carred the things to him james wescoat Brought him   I got
permission to go in and Se him   he was well and in verry
good spirits more so then I expected to find him   I was only
allowed 10 minutes to talk with him   he dont think they
will do much with him   he has not had his tryal yet   I will
be witness for him on his tryal all I can say for him   I can tel
them that Nat and my Self started Back at the preserdents
proclamation and I was Sick and he came back with me
and he intended going back to his Regemt and people tole
him that they was killing all the men that dident go Back at
the preserdents proclamation   Then he was fred to go back
and joe watson came down to fluvanna couty Recruting*

and nat an my Self concluded we would go with him as we thought that was a good chance   he Said that was all he wanted me to witnesS for him and I will do all I can for him   nat Said smith was inthere with him   I went to the Confedrate army and Saw aurelious   he and hiS famly iS well   He Sends his lov to you   he dident like the way mr mahone and Davidson treated you   He tole me all about it   I am verry Sorry to think you was treated So when I was absent from you   it certainly herts my feelings and dont you kear anything about it   no boddy wouldent treat you So but Som mean low life person and I will Remember them for that   I hope I willbe with you my Self before long and so is can protect you   Then no Boddy Shal not treat you mean   you wrote me word to let you know what diferculty I was in if I was alluding to tump smith   I don't consider that any diferculty at all   if that was all to get me in diferculty I would be free   I am not thinking about him   I havent herd anything about him   Since I came down hear all of them herd about it at the camp before I got hear and they all Said I don him Right   you need not be uneaSy about me   I am all Right as fare is that is concerned   you know I was in diferculty about being absent from my company So long   that was all but I hope that will not be much   I havent much news to write this time   Aurelious Says when ever you wantS to com to Richmond come to his house and you Shal be treated well is fare is he is able to treat you and you are welcom any Time you feel like coming and I know you is Two so don't you kear for no boddy and dont notice Such low life caricters as treated you So   I wouldent talk about them   we must not notice triffles now   if I was out of this war I wouldent care for no boddy   I could get along eaSy   you must be sure and write for me when you are

confind and I will be sure to com if I can and if I dont come
you must not think hard of it becaus you know I will come
if I can I want to Se you mighty bad but you know I cant
come now you are all of my thoughtS day and night you
are all in this world can make me happy and I never will
be happy no more in this world without you I anymore to
write thiS time write me word whether william is gone to
the army or no giv my Respects to him and his famly and
to perenton and hiS famly also and your mother and famly
alSo and Receiv my particular lov and Respects for your Self
I hope the time will [not] be long now before we will meat to
never part no more in thiS earth I hope we will meat in a
better world where pleasure never dies no more but Remains
your tru and loving husband untel death parts us from this
unfrendly world
M B Thurman
Co C 14th Va Regemt Bartons Brig pickits Division
In care leutenant Wm phrith
Write Soon

In Merit's letter to Jane of April 29, 1864, he mentioned
a problem with his arm. (Whatever it was, it must not have been
serious as his unit was drilling every day. With all of the different
"carry" positions used for the rifle-musket—and practiced during
drills—Merit's arm, whichever it was, would have gotten plenty
of exercise.) He then talked about traveling to Richmond for
his trial—under guard—the previous Friday. The trial was not
concluded, however, as all of the witnesses were not present. The
following Tuesday he was taken back to Richmond and all of
the witnesses were present. Nat was brought over from Castle
Thunder, evidently, but Merit did not say where they had to
go to get Jim Westcoat who had returned recently from being

AWOL.[10] The five witnesses Merit listed from his company were three privates, a second sergeant, and Lieutenant Frith who advised him not to mention that he had joined another company. Also, when they brought in Nat as a witness, he had his lawyer with him because he thought his trial was taking place. Merit noted that Nat was in good physical condition. Mr. Watson, who had recruited Nat and Merit while they were at home AWOL, wrote a letter on Nat's behalf as well. After the trial, Merit said he was back with his company "same as ever" although he had as yet to receive his sentence. Merit wrote that Jim Carver, a private from his company, was in Castle Thunder—handcuffed—and was living on bread and water. Merit wrote Carver's wife to tell her Jim's whereabouts, but not his circumstances.

Merit noted that the Yankees had advanced, and were within two miles of Bottom's Bridge where the 57th Regiment of Barton's Brigade was posted. Merit's 14th Virginia Infantry had been ordered to reinforce the 57th Virginia in the event of an attack. (Bottom's Bridge was located just east of Richmond on the South Anna River, near Quinton on present-day Route 249.)

In this note Merit referred to Jane's letter in which she had advised him to get ready to meet her in heaven if she never saw him again in this world. Merit, however, hoped to see her again on this earthly plain. (Jane was obviously extremely worried about her husband and he was attempting to console her. Since the two never saw each other again, one wonders if she had had a premonition of his death.)

Merit ended this letter with love for all his immediate family, Mr. Page and family, and Jane's brother, Perrington. He also told Jane to tell her sister, Ellen, that Nat looked "peart" and that he would testify for Nat at his trial. Merit's final message was that the Home Guards should be at the front if they could not stop people stealing from poor, unprotected women. (Merit wanted Jane to "find out if you can." Just what he meant is unclear. Perhaps it was either why the Home Guards were not more vigilant or if they were going to be assigned to the front. Stealing from the women back home was a real problem as Susan Gillespie wrote to her husband, Jackson that "rogues" were stealing from her. She declared she would shoot them if they came near.[11])

camp near Richmond april 29th 1864

My dear loving wife I Seat my Self to write to you onest more again as I Received jour kind affectionate letter yesterday and I was extreemly glad to hear from you i wiSh I could get a letter from you evry day for you are all the plesure that iS in thiS world for me I am well and hearty all to my arm but I can use it som. I am drilling evry day my dear Rosser I hope thiS may find you well and injoying all the good health and blessings god can afford you in thiS world my good little wife I would be the gladest in the world to Se you I waS carried to Richmond last friday to my tryal under gard but they did not finish trying me on account of not having all my witnesses so I was carried back to camp and Tuesday they had me there to tryal again and I had nat and jim wescoat summonds they sent to cassle thunder after nat and brought him to the court house and nat and jim don all they could for me and five of the men from the company waS ther too leutenant phrith william pace dick white henry bolls jim Richardson and they don all in favor of me I could expect for them to do I am now

at my company at duty aS Same as ever   I dont know what
my Sentence will be yet but I dont Recon it will be much
so you make your self contented about that   jim carver iS
put in cassle thunder for eight weeks and to be hand Kuffed
and fed on Bred and water during the time   I wrote a
letter to hiS wife yesterday that he waS in cassle thunder
for eight weeks but I dident Say anything about they hand
Kuffing and feeding him on bred and water and dont you
tel her becaus it will make her uneaSy and they may put
me in cassle thunder too for a little while but I dont think
they will becaus my charges was not as bad as jim carverS
they cant do much with me but if they do dont you trubble
your Self about it   they cant hert me much   the yankees
is advancing   they are in Two mile of bottomses Bridge
where the 57th Regement iS   Colnal white Received orders
last night to hold the 14th in Reddyness to Reinfoce if they
Should make an attact   I havent any mor news to write of
importance   tel Sister Ellen nat look verry well and waS
in good Spirits   he iS fatter then I ever Saw him   they will
not do much with him aS people thinkS when they brought
him to the court house to be witneSS for me he thought they
brought him up to hiS tryal and he brought hiS lawer with
hm   His lawer seem to pay mighty good attention to him
nat is got watsons letter   I dident tel them anything about
me joining another company   leutenant phrith advise me
not   i dont beleave I hav any more to write now   my dear
Rosser you wrote me word that I must try and prepare to
meat you in heven if you Should never Se me anymore in
this world   I wish I could   I know it iS good advice but I am
in hopes god will Spare us both to meat again in this world
before long to part no more untel death   then I hope we
will meat in heven where they say pleasure never dies   my

*sweet little wife you must not greave and trubble your Self
So much I know you do from the way you write and you
must not do so becauS it dont do any good I loves you just
as dearly aS I can love you and I hope it will not be long
befor we will I have an opotunity of doing better I am in
good Spirits yet and you make your Self contented becaus
I am coming to you again or die and tel Sister Ellen I am
going to do all I can for nat and i know I can do a great deel
in favor of him nat looks mighty peart and talkS big as
ever he lookS like he dont kear for nothing much tel her I
think nat will come out all write yet giv my best lov to your
mother and all the famly and mr page and famly also and
perinton I will writ to perinton in a day or two I think
the home gards had better come in the army wher they can
do Som good if they cant keep the people from Steeling from
the poor wimen that are left ther unpretected I want you to
find out if you can and let me no nothing more at present
But Remains your tru loving husband untel death parts us
from this world
M. B. Thurman
Co. C 14th Virginia Regmt
BartonS Brigde pickits division*

The following short, undated letter seems to fit in this
period because in it Merit asked Jane if she had heard anything
from the government. If not, he wrote, then he wanted her to ask
Doctor Boston to attend to it. (She was obviously trying to get
some help from the government of some kind. Most likely, Merit
wanted a furlough to come home and take care of his wife. These
are speculations of course. This letter may have been stuck in
another letter or written shortly after a previous one.)

my dear little RoSSer
I will write you a few more lineS.   write me word whether
the government is finding you anything or not   I want to
know and if they are not ask doctor Boston to attend to it for
you   I havent any more to write thiS time   you must write
to me Regular and let me hear from you   that is all the
pleasure I Se is to Read your letters   giv my best lov to your
mother and all the famly and all inquiring friends if there
be any   you must do the best you can   I hope it will not be
long before we will be together in peace   I lov you now better
then I ever did   I am willing To die for you   I cant say any
more then that   it herts my feelings to think I hav got a good
wife and a pretty wife then is to be in the fix I am in   I dont
intend to stand it if I can do any better   I means to get out
of this [or] die   nothing more for this time   write Soon as
you can
yours Sencearly
M B Thurman
company C   14th Virginia Regemt

Merit's brother, Robert, penned the following to Jane
on April 30, 1864. In it he mentioned that he had received a
letter from Merit a few days earlier and that Merit was well.
(The letters back and forth between the Thurman brothers
demonstrated close family ties.)

Robert had taken part in a religious revival in his camp
at Madison Run during the early months of 1864. Chaplain
Hilary E. Hatcher reported a revival in Mahone's Brigade—of
which Robert's regiment was a part—in August and September
of 1863.[12] Hatcher wrote that it had been six months since
Mahone's men had heard a sermon, although they had been

assembling regularly for prayer.[13] He noted that on September 10, 1863, 146 men had found peace in Christ.[14] Chaplain William J. Jones wrote that on February 21, 1864, he preached to a large number of Mahone's men and that Bible classes and prayer meetings were being held in nearly every company in the brigade.[15] Chaplain L. C. Vass reported on March 23, 1864, that the revival in Mahone's Brigade was continuing with 140 professions of conversion in three of its regiments.[16] Chaplain Pugh had a full-fledged revival going on in the early months of 1864 at the camp near Madison Run Station.[17]

Robert wrote Jane that they had a fine "meeting" in their camp, and that he had been baptized the previous Sunday. Robert noted that it would be good news to hear that Merit had made his peace with God. He also urged Jane to do so if she had not already. Robert intended to write Merit the following day and, no doubt, would encourage him to draw closer to God. (Robert was becoming quite an evangelist.)

During the winter of 1863–4, fifteen-day furloughs were given to soldiers with the hope it would improve their morale.[18] Robert evidently visited with his brother Aurelius and his wife Nannie in Richmond. Robert was very upset because he felt Nannie had treated his mother "worse than a dog" while they were living with her. He wrote Jane that he did not like Nannie because of what she had done. Robert was also upset that Aurelius had not taken Jane to see Merit when she was in the capital. He was also sorry to hear that Jane was "unwell." (Perhaps this was a reference to her pregnancy.)

Camp 41st Va Infantry
April 30th 1864

Dear Sister

your letter of the 24th was gladly Received the 28th I was
glad to hear from you and to hear you were well this leaves
me in good health and hope it may find you enjoying the
Same blessing there is no war news about here We is quiet
at this and I hope it Stay So oh I would Be glad if this
cruel war would come to a close But I fear there is many of
us that will have to mingle with the dust Before this cruel
war is Settled I have just been looking(?) at your letter
...........where you said you is unwell I am Very Sorry to
hear that But I hope this will find you well I am Very Sorry
you did not See Merit when you was in Richmond I know
he would have been glad to have Seen you I think it was
as little as Aureliss could have done to lost one dayS work
and went after Merit But those that are not in the army
cares But cares little about those that are in it I See enough
action when I was at aureliuses on furlough yes enough to
Satisfy me about him and his wife I can tell you I tell you
Some things that you ever did Be Surprised to hear my
dear old mother was treated worse than a dog By nannie
But I dont want you to Say any thing about it when merit
knows all about it Aurelius and nannie having done for
me did they Say any thing about me to you after I came
from Richmond I wrote to aurelius about how mother
was treated and he wrote me a Very insulting letter I have
not answered his letter and I dont know if I Shall write to
him any more I gave him to understand that I did not like
nannie and he Said any one that was not a friend to her was
no friend of his of course he dont consider me any friend
of his I am wiling to do anything for him that I can But
if he chooses to think that I am an enemy of his I cant help
it I am no enemy of his it is my wish to Be friendly with

every Body we have a fine meeting in our camp thank god
I have a hope of meeting you all in heaven I was Baptised
last Sunday I wish merit was a christian it was Be good
news if I could just hear that [he] had made peace with god
oh who could die a Sinner Dear Sister I would like to know
whether you a profesor of Religion or not if you are not
don't put it of you must die and you cant tell how long you
will live you may never live to See the Riseing of another
Sun and I hope to meet you in heaven and if we don't love
and Serve god here we cant expect to go where he is in
heaven give my love to all the family and Receive the Same
for yourself from your ever devoted Brother until death
Robert H Thurman
good Bye
write Soon

[Upside down on top of letter]
Grandison and Beverly Send there Best love to you I
Receive a letter from merit a few days ago he was well I
will write to him tomorrow if nothing happens to prevent
me from So doing it is geting late So I will come to a close
Nothing more at present write Soon

Merit penned the following correspondence on May 5, 1864. In preparation for the probable movements of the Army of the Potomac, the 14th Virginia—along with "all of Barton's Brigade" according to Merit—had marched to Hanover Junction where they were guarding the South Anna Bridge on the Fredericksburg Railroad. Even as they marched to the junction from Richmond, the Federal forces under General Grant had crossed the Rapidan River and were heading south toward a major confrontation in the Wilderness with the Army of Northern Virginia under General Lee. Also, on May 5 the Army of the James under Union Maj. Gen. Benjamin F. Butler—numbering about 36,000 men—left Fort Monroe for Bermuda Hundred below Richmond in order to drive a wedge between Petersburg and Richmond and cut the railroad in that area.

Merit wrote Jane that he had received a "mighty good letter" from his brother saying that Robert had "profest Religion and bin baptised." In it Robert had advised him to "get religion" as well. (The war was dragging on, the casualty lists were mounting, and Robert was extremely concerned about his brother's spiritual well-being.)

Merit noted that he saw Davidson while in Richmond and that Davidson apologized for his bad treatment of Jane. Davidson—who was married to Merit's sister, Mariah—claimed that he had only been joking. Mariah must have been sick as Merit said that she "can just walk a little."

Merit wrote that he and Jane "will hav to part for awhile"—perhaps meaning they will have to remain apart—and he did not know what would become of him. He wanted her to know, however, that he not only loved her in this life, but would love her after death. (One wonders if he had had a premonition of his coming death.)

Camp near hanover junction
may 5th 1864 My dear wife

My dear Rosser I take my pen in hand to write to you onest more as I have an opotunity to let you hear from me I am

*well aS comon and hopes when those few lines comes to hand
they may find you will and injoying all the good blessings
ans health god can afford you in this world we are now in
camp near hanover junction in Site of mr greens house in
a mile of The Same place we was when you was hear we
left Richmond day before yesterday we are garding the
Southhaner Bridge on the fredericksburg Railroad and
Severel other places to prevent the yankees from making
Rode threw hear the yankee army iS thiS Side of the
Rapedan River all of bartons Brigade is hear I havent
much news To write this time I got a letter from Robert
yesterday he has profest Religion and bin baptised he
wrote me a mighty good letter he advised me to try and get
Religion he Said he got a letter from you a few days ago
and Said he would be mighty glad to Se you he Says he
knows you iS a good woman from the way you writes to him
and I Saw davidson when I was at Richmond he made all
apolegise to me he could about treating you as he did he
Said he was just joking with you he Said he thought more
of you then any woman he ever Saw dont mind him he
iS not much no how I was at hiS house mariah just can
walk a little he iS mighty trifeling but he iS doing a little
better then he waS I am of the same mind I was when I left
home I Recon we will hav to part for awhile though I may
continue for a while at the Sam old post but I don't know
what will become of me yet but you do the best you can I
will be able to do Somthing for you before long if I liv So
you make your self contented the best you can. I hope god
will Spare uS to meat again to never part no more I think
a heep about you you are my hole Studdy I love you better
then evry thing in the world I will lov you aS long iS I live
I will lov you untel I die and lov you after I am dead no*

more but Remains your loving husband untel death part uS
then I hope we will meat in heven where parting iS no more
M B Thurman to my dear good wife j. R. T.

Merit's last letter to Jane was dated May 6, 1864. He
wrote that he had received a letter from her on the day he had
written her last. (According to the Supplement to the Official
Records, Company C, 14th Virginia left Hanover Junction
the might of May 7 and arrived at Drewry's Bluff by rail the
morning of May 8.[19]) Merit noted that there had been an awful
fight at Orange Court House "a few days ago" and that there
were a great number killed on both sides. He said that it was a
complete slaughter and he hoped his brothers and cousin were
not killed. (The date of Merit's letter has to be in error, however,
as the terrible fighting at the Wilderness did not begin until
May 5.[20] From what he wrote about, and from the company
record, the letter's correct date must be May 8.) Merit's brothers,
and a cousin, were in the 41st Virginia, which did not get into
the battle until May 6.[21] According to Merit, Barton's Brigade
was now eight miles north of Petersburg in line of battle facing
Butler's Army of the James.

In the following Merit tried to prepare Jane for his
possible death. He would do his best to take care of himself, he
said, but if he should be killed, she must do the best that she
could. His statement "what iS to be will be and we cant help
it" was obviously a reference to his belief in predestination. He
did not want to die, however, and leave his wife behind. He just
wanted the war to be over and did not care which side won.
Evidently, Jane had written that she needed him to send her
money. He replied that he probably would not get paid until the
worst fighting was over. He said that he saw trouble ahead for Jane.

Merit asked Jane to remember him to Mr. Page and
Perrington, and their families, so neither had as yet been
conscripted. Nat had still not been tried, (but he must have
been returned to his company at some point as he was captured
in the fall of 1864.)[22] Merit wrote that "moses desper and sam
morse is sentenced to stay in prison for six months." (The service
records for these two men are interesting in that both evidently
hating camping in winter. William Moses Desper was AWOL
from December 28, 1862, until February 18, 1863, and deserted
December 28, 1863 until February 18, 1864 when he was
arrested.[23] Samuel J. Moss deserted August 16, 1862, and did not
rejoin his company until February 18, 1864.[24] Since they both
came back or were arrested on the same date, they may have been
together.)

Finally, Merit asked Jane to pray for him because he
wanted to live to see her again. He wrote that he did not mind
dying except for leaving Jane behind. (Merit may have taken his
brother's advice and made a commitment to Christ, or "gotten
religion" as they referred to conversion in those days.)

chesterfield County
may the 6th 1864

*My dear lovly wife I Seat my Self to write a few lines to
you I Received your letter the same day after I wrote to you
and was truly glad to hear from you this leavs me tolerable
well at thiS time we are in chesterfield now in a line of
battle we com hear last night Started about one oclock
_____ all the time we
can hear them fighting now down below uS we are now in
eight miles of petersburg I am going to do the best I can for*

my Self but if I Should get killed you muSt do the best you can   what iS to be will be and we cant help it but I hope that will not be   I dont want to get killed and leav my good little wife behind   the iS hard times in the army now but I hope it will not be long before the war will be ended one way ore the other   you wrote me word to write you word when I would know[?] any money   I cant tel you   I dont know   I dont Recon they will pay off untel the worse fighting is over they had a awful fight at ornange court house a few days ago I hope my brothers and cuzon did not get killed but they Say the was a great many killed on both Sides   they Say it was a compleet Slaugter   my dear make your Self contented and dont greav no more then you can help   I Se a hepse of trubble about you   I cant treat you good like I want to treat you   you is So good to me   I know I hav got the best wife in the world and I hope god will Spare us to meat together onest more to never part no more on earth   I havent time to write any more   it iS geting dark now   giv my best lov to your mother and all the famly and to mr page and his famly and perenton and hiS famly   nat iS not had his tryal yet moSeS deSper and Sam morse iS sentenced to stay in prison for six months   my dear loving little wife I havent any more to write So good by for this time   I hope I will liv to Se you again   you must pray for me   I wouldent mind dying So much if it want for leaving my good and pretty wife behind me   no more but Remains your tru and loving husband untel death   yourS Sincearly
M. B. Thurman   direct your letter to Richmond
14th Regemt BartonS Brigade
Pickets division

Chapter 6 Endnotes

1   Boatner, p. 433.
2   Crews and Parrish, p. 116.
3   Ibid., p. 105.
4   Ibid., p. 93.
5   Ibid., p. 144.
6   Hewitt, p. 372.
7   Crews and Parrish, p. 93.
8   Boatner, p. 749.
9   Sublett, p. 86.
10   Crews and Parrish, p. 150.
11   Miyagawa, p. 26–27.
12   J. William Jones, *Christ in the Camp* (Richmond, 1887), p. 330.
13   Ibid., p. 329.
14   Ibid., p. 330.
15   Ibid., p. 363.
16   Ibid., p. 373.
17   Henderson, p. 56.
18   Ibid.
19   Hewett, p. 372.
20   Henderson, p. 57.
21   Ibid., p. 59.
22   Sublett, p. 47.
23   Crews and Parrish, p. 99.
24   Ibid., p. 124.

Chapter 7:

Death of a Soldier

On May 10, 1864, Maj. Gen. Robert Ransom had two brigades under his command near Chester Station below Richmond—those of Brig. Gen. Archibald Gracie and Brig. Gen. Seth Barton. Ransom, in attempting to find the enemy's position, decided to order a reconnaissance in force. On his right the 14th Virginia Infantry advanced as skirmishers through the dense forest with the rest of Barton's Brigade deployed to the rear.[1] Gracie's Brigade moved forward on Barton's left. On Barton's front, coordination between his regiments was made even more difficult when the woods caught fire. Despite Barton's initial success against the enemy—posted in a large clearing around the Winfree house—Federal reinforcements arrived in time to stop the Southern drive.

General Barton made the following report on the 14th Virginia's part in the battle under Col. William White: "While the advance of the left had proceeded so well, White dashed his line of skirmishers over an open field for about 1,000 yards against a battery supported by a strong line of infantry (at least a

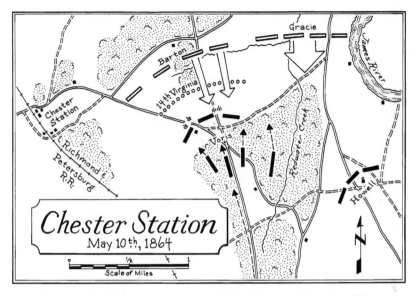

Map illustrating battle lines as they were likely drawn at the battle of Chester Station, in the vicinity of Richmond, VA. Map drawn by Rick Britton.

brigade), but was unable to take it, though he silenced the guns and drove the enemy from the open ground. Heavy forces of the enemy were brought forward and he was forced to retire. Halting in his original position and resting for a few moments, he again advanced at the charge and retook the position first gained. The morass on his left made it necessary for him to double his line there and prevented Col. W. R. Aylett (who commanded the 53rd Virginia) from connecting closely. Aylett's advance had left a part of the enemy's line between the two regiments, and a heavy fire on the rear and flanks of both followed. White retired his left to face it, and Aylett his right for the same purpose. Reinforcements came to both flanks and front to the enemy, thus nearly encompassing the three left regiments and forcing the line back slowly and reluctantly. The whole retired in good order."[2]

The report of Company C, 14th Virginia Infantry—
Merit's company—is as follows: "Engaged the enemy in the
morning near Chester Station. The company behaved well,
having made two desperate charges on the enemy line of battle;
lost one man killed and four wounded. Moved back in the same
evening to the line of fortifications where we remained."[3]

In the action at Chester Station, Barton's Brigade suffered
a total of 249 casualties.[4] Of those, the 14th Virginia lost the
most men, seventy-one, which included twelve men killed, two
officers and forty-two men wounded, and fifteen men missing.[5]

After Barton's withdrawal, both sides declared a truce to
rescue the wounded men who lay in the path of the forest fire
raging around the crossroads. Unfortunately, they were unable to
save all of the wounded from the flames.[6]

The one man killed in Company C was Meredith "Merit"
Branch Thurman. The muster report of his company for May and
June of 1864 reported Merit killed in action on May 10, 1864.
One can only hope that he was not burned to death after being
wounded.

Through Merit's wonderful letters, we have experienced
the poignant life story of an ordinary Southern enlisted man.
Stories like Merit's are rare because families usually refrain
from revealing that their ancestors went AWOL or deserted
from the Confederate Army. Despite his absences from the
ranks, however, Merit Branch Thurman was a good soldier.
This we know from the testimony of his regimental colonel, the
lieutenant commanding his company, and his fellow comrades-
in-arms.

His family can be proud of him, as well as of his brothers, who fought to defend the state of Virginia from the invading Northern Army. The South's cause may have been wrong and unjust, but the stance taken by the Thurman boys was noble. Merit was pulled in two different directions during the war—he was torn between his devotion to his wife and his devotion to his country. He was torn between Love and Duty.

Chapter 7 Endnotes

1   William Glenn Robertson, *Back Door to Richmond* (Baton Rouge, 1987), p. 124.
2   Crews and Parrish, p. 52.
3   Hewitt, p. 372.
4   Crews and Parrish, p. 52.
5   Ibid.
6   Robertson, p. 127.

Appendix 1:
A Brother's Consoling Letter

In the following letter to Jane, Robert Thurman tried to console her in the loss of her husband. At the same time he was grieving over the loss of his brother. He attempted to convince her to live as a Christian and, if he too were killed, he hoped to meet her in heaven. Robert had received letters on the same day from both Merit and Jane, and said that he would treasure Merit's as long as he lived. (Unfortunately, Merit's letter to Robert did not survive the war.) Robert wrote Jane that she will always be regarded as his sister and that he will not forget her.

Near Hanover Junction
May 22, 1864

Dear Sister
I take the pleasure of answering your letter which came
to me about a week ago   I would have answered it Before
now But we have marching and part of the time fighting
every day Since the 6 of this month   Dear Sister it was sad
to hear that my dear Brother was killed But I hope he was
a changed man Before the lord called him to himself   Dear
Sister we must try and Bare this troubles   the lord giveth
and the lord taketh   Blessed Be the name of the lord   my
dear Brother is gone   we will never See him again in this
world So we must prepare to meet him in heaven   I hope
he is there out of this troubled world where there is no wars

*or troubles for us   Dear Sister I hope you will Bare this loss
of your devoted Husband   it is hard to loose one that is so
near and dear to us But we must Remember it is the lords
will   I Received a letter from him the day I Received yours
and that letter as long as I live   I hope you will try and live
a christian and if we should never meat in this world to try
and meat in heaven   I have Been _____
we had a friend killed and 8 wounded   Beverly is wounded
But not Bad   But thank god I am yet unhirt   Grandison
and myself has come out unhirt so fore and I hope the lord
will protect us through all dangers   we were out thir risking
nearly all day yesterday   my Co. had one man wounded
our Regiment had several killed and wounded   Dear Sister
I would write you a long letter But the Bad yankees is
constant shelling us   I am now in our intrenchments   give
my Best Respects to your maw Fannie and Receive my Best
love for yoursef   from your ever devoted
Brother R. H. Thurman
Upside down at top of second page:*

*Dear Sister I will ever love you as a sister and I hope I may
Be Spared to have the pleasure of visiting you as a sister   I
will never forsake you But will always love you and I hope
you will love me as a Brother   dont think you will Be
forgotten   I will always Remember you   good Bye
Soon*

Appendix 2:

Perrington's Letter to Sister Caroline

The following letter was written after the war by Jane's brother Perrington (P. H. H.), to their sister, Caroline (Mrs. C. V. Thomas of Albemarle County, Virginia). (It's the last one of the copies I possess and was included because it described both Caroline's and Perrington's faith. Caroline may have married the Jack Thomas mentioned in Merit's letter of April 7, 1864, as having just returned to the army.)

Perrington was in very bad health—evidently dying of consumption, the term then-used for tuberculosis. Perrington looked on his affliction as sent from God. It was helpful to him, he noted, from a "spiritual point of view." Perrington urged Caroline to keep her faith in God and he hoped she would recover and be useful to God's church. Perrington hoped that he might get well enough to come and see Caroline. It was an encouraging letter (despite his idea that God afflicts us).

What was important in this letter was that Perrington referred to "Mother Ross." When Perrington last saw Caroline, she had urged him to talk to "Mother Ross and all to try to prepare to meet you in heaven." "Ross" evidently said that she was coming up to see Caroline and may have arrived the evening this letter was written. (It seems strange that Perrington called

his sister Jane "Mother Ross"—perhaps that was his nickname
for her—but it was obviously Jane that he referred to.) Little
Anna Jane was now almost seven years old and could travel with
her mother. It was good of Jane to visit her siblings who were in
such bad health. Finally, Perrington said to tell Mrs. Harlow and
Mrs. Brooks that if he got well enough, he would visit and let
them fatten him. Perrington's mother was still living as he added
a note to her at the end of this letter. (Perrington was quite an
evangelist in telling everyone to get ready for heaven. No one
knows when the Son of Man is coming.)

april 25 1871

Dear Sister Caroline
it has been Some time Since we Saw each other   it has been
the will of God to afflict both of us with the same dreadful
disease Consumption. but I hope each of us Can Say it is
good for us that we have been afflicted, in a Spiritual point
of view.   I feel it is the Cace with me and I trust it is the
Same with you from what you Said to me when we last
parted begging me to talk with Mother Ross and all to try
to prepare to meet you in heaven.   I trust you have been
faithful and Still look to that friend that Sticketh closer than
a brother.   My Dear Sister you must look to god for help.
he will Stand by you when all earthly help Shall fail   Spend
much of your time in prayer and O for the Lords Sake try
and be prepared when death Shall Come that you may be
free from all your Sufferings and go to that place where there
is no SickneSs , Sorrow, pain nor death, but where Joy and
gladneSs Shall forever reign.   I trust that we may live each
day as tho it were our last and if it is the will of god that we
Should never meet again on earth I hope we will meet in

heaven I trust in the lord that he will raise you from your bed of affliction to a life of usefulneSs to his Church. how glad I would be to See you   I hope the lord will restore me to a little better health So as I Can Come up and See you all. I am not as well as I have been my legs and arms is very sore but I can walk out a little Ann is Complaining has been for several days but keeps up the most of the time She Says She is coming up and See you all as Soon as She can you must give our best love to Jack, Mother Ann's Mother Mrs Brooks and tell them to try and be ready for death for the son of man cometh at an hour that we think not I must Close as I do not feel much like writing from your devoted Brother   P. H. Humphrey

PS
Dear Mother I expect RoSs has gone up this eve to See you all She was here this morning ans Spoke of going if She has not. They are all as well as Common do not be uneasy about home now me if any thing happens we will let you know tell Mrs Harlow and Mrs Brooks if I get well enough I am coming up for them to fatten me. your affectionate Son
P. H. H
On envelope: Mrs C. V. Thomas
Ashton albemarle
Va

Appendix 3:
The Family after Merit's Death

First Sergeant Robert Hezekiah Sublett Thurman of
Company D, 41st Virginia Infantry, Mahone's Brigade, was
killed in action at the Battle of the Crater on July 30, 1864. The
account of Robert's death was told as follows by Maj. William
Etheridge of the 41st Virginia: "I was among the first to jump
into the ditch where the Yanks were as thick as they could stand.
The first sergeant of Co. D jumped in about the same time as I
did, and was killed instantly."[1]

Grandison Woodson Thurman, Company D, 41st
Virginia Infantry, Mahone's Brigade, was illiterate (which is
why we have no letters from him). Grandison was captured at
Burgess's Mill—also known as Hatcher's Run—on October 27,
1864, and interned at Point Lookout Prison in Maryland from
October 31, 1864, until June 21, 1865, when he took the Oath of
Allegiance and was released.[2]

Nathaniel D. Bacon of Company H, 57th Virginia
Infantry, Barton's Brigade, was captured at Front Royal on
October 11, 1864, and interned at Point Lookout Prison
in Maryland until May 12, 1865, when he took the Oath of
Allegiance and was released.[3]

Beverly Ammonett, Company D, 41st Virginia Infantry,
Mahone's Brigade, survived his wounding at the Wilderness and

was paroled in Richmond on April 30, 1865.[4]

Aurelius Daniel Thurman of Company B, 1st Battalion, Virginia Infantry, Local Defense Force, was paroled in April of 1865 and died shortly afterwards in a Richmond hospital.[5]

George Mills Thurman, Company G, 12th North Carolina Infantry, North Carolina Volunteers, was one of Merit's older brothers. He was not mentioned by Merit since he was in a regiment from another state. He survived the war and was married to Louisa Graham. He died in Jonesboro, Arkansas, in 1882.

Jane Rosser Humphrey Thurman gave birth to Anna Jane Thurman on June 19, 1864. She had two additional children, Addie J. Thurman (born May 17, 1866, in Fluvanna County), and Orvid R. Thurman (born January 10, 1867, in Fluvanna County). No father's name was listed. In 1865, Jane sold eighty-seven acres of land for $100. On December 29, 1874, Jane married James H. Beach, a miller, who was a widower. James and Jane had several children.

Appendix 4:

The Fluvanna County Census of 1850 and the Humphrey Family

The 1850 census record for Fluvanna County (p. 102–103) lists the Royal Winston Humphrey family as follows:

Mary Humphrey	39 years	Female
Julia Humphrey	21 years	Female
Elizabeth Humphrey	19 years	Female
Perrington Humphrey	17 years	Male
Irene Humphrey	14 years	Female
Caroline Humphrey	11 years	Female
Nancy E. Humphrey	8 years	Female
Jane Humphrey	6 years	Female

The Fluvanna County Land Book for 1844–1850, lists Royal Winston Humphrey as buying 400 acres in 1844. In the Fluvanna County Certificates of Marriage Book of 1781–1849 (on page 130), a certificate of marriage dated September 24, 1827, is listed for Royal W. Humphrey and Mary Jane Harlowe. Also, the Fluvanna County Court Orders for 1840–1847 (on page 110), says Royal Humphrey was granted a certificate for obtaining letters of administration of his father Bartlett Humphrey's estate. Since Royal is not mentioned in the 1850 census, we can only assume that he had passed away sometime after 1844 when he bought the 400 acres. We can also assume that the land Jane sold in 1865 was her inheritance from her father.

Appendix 5:
Family Bible Record of Hezekiah B. and Nancy Thurman's Children[6]

~

1. Daniel Lewis Thurman was born Thursday 15th September 1814.
2. Wm. Decatur Thurman was born Wednesday 3rd April 1816.
3. George Mills Thurman was born Monday 18th May 1818. (He was married in 1841, in Campbell Co., Va., to Louisa Graham. He died 1882, in Craighead Co., Ark. He served in the CSA.)
4. Elisa Ann Thurman was born Saturday 7th October 1820. (She married 1846, in Chesterfield Co., Va., James Ketton.)
5. Grandison Woodson Thurman was born Thursday 26th December 1822. (He married Ann Brown in 1846, and Maria L. Hall in 1857. He served in the Confederate Army.)
6. Merit Branch Thurman was born Friday 29th April 1825.
7. John Beverly Thurman was born Sunday 2nd Sept. 1827. (He married 1845, in Chesterfield Co., Va., Nancy Ann Scyre. He died 1859, in a mine explosion in Chesterfield Co.)
8. Mariah Oney Thurman was born Friday 2nd April 1830. (She married 1849, in Chesterfield Co., Va., John L. Kiper.)
9. Robert Hezekiah Sublett Thurman was born Saturday Sept 1st 1832. (He fought for the Confederacy and died in the Battle of the Crater.)

10. Aurelious Daniel Thurman was born Tuesday 30th June 1835. (He was in the CSA. He died shortly after being paroled in April 1865, while in a Richmond hospital.)

Daniel Lewis Thurman departed this life March 5th 1835 aged 20 years and 5 months and 18 days.

Hezekiah Bowles Thurman departed this life January 6th 1840.

Nancy Thurman moved to Winterfield to live the 5th day of August 1840. (She was listed in the 1860 Chesterfield Co. census.)

William Decatur and Permelia Catharine Roberts Thurman were preceded to Fayette Co. by some of her family.

Appendix 6:
Thurman Family Genealogy

A descendent of George Mills Thurman, Paul Wharton, has done extensive work in putting together a genealogy of the Thurman family using records from Chesterfield County in Virginia, Storey County in Nevada, and Daniel Lewis Thurman's Bible which Joanne Moore used in her article in Appendix V. It is as follows:

Husband: Hezekiah Bowles Thurman
      Born: 1796 in Chesterfield County, VA
      Died: January 6, 1840 in Chesterfield County, VA
      Married: April 14, 1813 in Chesterfield Count, VA
Wife: Ann "Nancy" McGrudder
      Born: 1796 in Chesterfield County, VA
      Died: September 10, 1863 in Richmond, VA

Children:
1. Daniel Lewis Thurman
      Born: September 15, 1814 in Chesterfield County, VA
      Died: March 5, 1835 in Chesterfield County, VA
      Unmarried
2. William Decatur Thurman
      Born: April 3, 1816 in Chesterfield County, VA
      Died: 1886 in Fayette County, TN
      Married: February 16, 1846 in Chesterfield County, VA
      Spouse: Permelia Roberts

3. George Mills Thurman
> Born: May 18, 1818 in Chesterfield County, VA
> Died: May 8, 1882 in Jonesboro, AK
> Married: February 3, 1841 in Lynchburg, Campbell County, VA
> Spouse: Louisa Graham

4. Eliza Ann Thurman
> Born: October 7, 1820 in Chesterfield County, VA
> Died: March 1897 in Storey County, NV
> Buried: March 16, 1897 in Gold Hill Cemetery
> Married: May 11, 1846 in Chesterfield County, VA
> Spouse: James M. Ketton

5. Grandison Woodson Thurman
> Born: December 26, 1822 in Chesterfield County, VA
> Died: Before 1900
> Married #1: December 7, 1846 in Chesterfield County, VA
> Spouse: Ann Brown
> Married #2: September 25, 1857
> Spouse: Mariah Elliott Hall (widow)

6. Merritt Branch Thurman
> Born: April 26, 1825 in Chesterfield County, VA
> Died: May 10, 1864 in Chesterfield County (Battle of Chester Station)
> Married: December 2, 1862 in Fluvanna County. VA
> Spouse: Jane Rosser Humphrey

7. John Beverly Thurman
> Born: September 2, 1827 in Chesterfield County, VA
> Died: June 1877 in Storey County, NV
> Buried: June 18, 1877 in Gold Hill Cemetery
> Married: March 1, 1854 in Chesterfield County, VA
> Spouse: Caroline Louisa Condrey

8. Mariah Oney Thurman
       Born: April 2, 1830 in Chesterfield County, VA
       Died: Date and place unknown
       Married #1: May 14, 1849 in Chesterfield County, VA
       Spouse: John L. Kiper
       Married #2: December 1856
       Spouse: Reuben P. Davidson
9. Robert Hezekiah Sublett Thurman
       Born: September 10, 1832 in Chesterfield County, VA
       Died: July 30, 1864 in Petersburg (Battle of the Crater)
       Unmarried
10. Aurelius Daniel Thurman
       Born: June 20, 1835 in Chesterfield County, VA
       Died: 1865 shortly after paroled in Richmond Hospital
       Married: December 23, 1862 in Richmond, VA
       Spouse: Nancy White

Appendices Endnotes

1   Alan Axelrod, *The Horrid Pit* (New York, 2007), p. 211.
2   Henderson, p. 142.
3   Sublett, p. 47.
4   Henderson, p. 86.
5   Joanne Cullom Moore, "Baugh-Roberts-Thurman," *Ansearchin' News* (Memphis, The Tennessee Genealogical Society), vol. 39, no. 4, p. 148.
6   Moore, p. 147–48.

Bibliography

Author Anonymous. Jerusalem Baptist Church (Winfree Memorial Baptist Church, 1981).

Axelrod, Alan. *The Horrid Pit*. (New York: Carroll and Graf Publishers, 2007).

Boatner, Mark Mayo. *The Civil War Dictionary*. (New York: David McKay Company, Inc., 1959).

Crews, Edward R. and Parrish, Timothy A. *14th Virginia Infantry*. (Lynchburg, VA: H. E. Howard, Inc., 1995).

Driver, Robert J., Jr. *5th Virginia Cavalry*. (Lynchburg, VA: H. E. Howard, Inc., 1997).

Druyvesteyn, Kent. "With Great Vision: The James River and Kanawha Canal," *Virginia Cavalcade*, vol. 21, no. 3. (Winter, 1972).

Freeman, Douglas Southhall. *Lee's Lieutenants,* vol. III. (New York: Charles Scribner's Sons, 1944).

Georg, Kathleen R. and Busey, John W. *Nothing But Glory: Pickett's Division at Gettysburg.* (Hightstown, N J: Longstreet House, 1987).

Henderson, William D. *41st Virginia Infantry.* (Lynchburg, VA: H. E. Howard, Inc., 1986).

Hewitt, Janet B., ed. *Supplement to the Official Records of the Union and Confederate Armies*, vol. 71 (Wilmington, NC: Broadfoot Publishing Company, 1998).

Jones, J. William. *Christ in the Camp.* (Richmond, VA: B. F. Johnson and Co., 1887).

Jones, Newton Bond. "Charlottesville and Albemarle County, Virginia, 1819-1860." (U.Va. Dissertation, 1950).

McGehee, Minnie Lee. "Old Mills of Fluvanna," *The Bulletin of the Fluvanna Historical Society*, nos. 10 and 11, (Palmyra, VA: The Fluvanna County Historical Society, 1970).

McGehee, Minnie Lee and Trout, William E. *Mr. Jefferson's River: The Rivanna.* (Charlottesville, VA: The Van Doren Co., 2001).

Miyagawa, Ellen, ed. *Fluvanna History: Dear Susan.* (Palmyra, VA: Seven Islands Company, 2004).

Miyagawa, Ellen. "The James River and Kanawha Canal in
    Fluvanna," *The Bulletin of the Fluvanna Historical
    Society*, no. 33, (Palmyra, VA: The Fluvanna
    County Historical Society, 1982).

Moore, Joanne Cullom. "Baugh-Roberts-Thurman"
    Ansearrhin News, vol. 39, no. 4. (Winter, 1992).

Motts, Wayne. *Trust in God and Fear Nothing: Gen. Lewis A.
    Armistead, CSA.* (Gettysburg: Farnsworth House
    Military Impressions, 1994).

Robertson, James I. Jr. Communication, November 19, 2008.

Robertson, William Glenn. *Back Door to Richmond.* (Baton
    Rouge: Louisiana State University Press, 1987).

Ruffner, Kevin C. *44th Virginia Infantry.* (Lynchburg, VA:
    H. E. Howard, Inc., 1987).

Sublett, Charles W. *57th Virginia Infantry.* (Lynchburg, VA:
    H. E. Howard, Inc., 1985).

Trout, W. E. and Runge, Peter C. *The Rivanna Scenic River
    Atlas.* (Richmond, VA: The Virginia Canals and
    Navigations Society, Revised Edition, 2002).

Weaver, Bettie Woodson. "The Mines of Midlothian,"
    Virginia Cavalcade, vol. 11, no. 3 (Winter, 1961-62).

Acknowledgements

There were many persons who helped me craft these letters into a book for future generations. I am thankful to my late Aunt Ethel Moran who originally showed me the letters she had borrowed from her aunt. At my request she read them and wrote an important sentence or two from each before she returned them.

My cousin, Katherine Shortlidge, to whom the letters had been passed down, made copies of each letter for me. When I could not discern some of the words, I would ask for her help. She was successful much of the time and she did all of this while working as a school teacher, as well as at a part-time job, to put her husband through medical school. Obviously, without her help, this book would not have been possible.

I am also thankful to my cousin, Jim Moran, who had all of the letters typed from my handwritten copies. Two other cousins who also had letters shared them with me. I am also thankful for their encouragement in producing this book.

The Albemarle and Fluvanna County Historical Societies were helpful in finding books for me. The Rockbridge Regional Library, the Preston Library at the Virginia Military Institute, and the Leyburn Library of Washington and Lee University provided access to books on regimental histories and the canals in central Virginia.

Discussions with Dr. Holt Merchant, the head of the History Department at Washington and Lee University, were always helpful in providing background information on Southern culture and the armies of both sides during the Civil War. He also reviewed the book and made extensive suggestions. His encouragement and excitement about the production of this book were also helpful.

Dr. James I. Robertson of the History Department at Virginia Polytechnic Institute and State University reviewed the book with several important suggestions that were very helpful.

Frank Grizzard, a local historian, gave me encouragement several times, telling me that if I did a little work on the book everyday, I could finish it in six months. I followed his advice and it really was helpful.

I am indebted to Robert E. L. Krick, the historian of the Richmond National Battlefield Park, for referring me to the *Supplements of the Official Records of the Union and Confederate Armies* and answering various questions for me as well as his encouragement to me in the preparation of this book.

My son, Mark Allen Crewdson and his wife, Judy, were very helpful to me with their computer expertise in dealing with computer problems I had in the process of working on this book.

My wife, Lois Ellen Crewdson, gave me continuous

encouragement as I worked on the book each day for many days in late 2007 and continuing through the spring of 2008.

Finally, I am indebted to Rick Britton who did an excellent job of editing my manuscript so that it is very readable. He also made original maps of Pickett's Charge and the battle of Chester Station for this book, showing where the 14th Virginia Regiment was involved.

The Author

The Reverend Dr. Robert Henry Crewdson is a retired Episcopal priest who has spent most of his ministry in rural and mountain parishes. He is a 1955 graduate of Virginia Polytechnic Institute and State University with a bachelor of science degree in chemical engineering. After working for a short time for the Dupont Company, he volunteered for the U.S. Navy and served as a hospital corpsman on the USS *Orion*, a submarine tender. He is a 1960 graduate of Virginia Theological Seminary with a master of divinity degree. He also holds master of sacred theology and doctor of ministry degrees from Union Theological Seminary in Richmond, Virginia.

Dr. Crewdson began studying the Civil War while in elementary school in Front Royal, Virginia, where he grew up. In his childhood, he could not help noticing the gray historical signs in Front Royal about Confederate Gen. Thomas Jonathan "Stonewall" Jackson's 1862 campaign in the Shenandoah Valley. So, when his fifth grade teacher asked her students to read a book and write a report on it, he chose a book about the life of Jackson. Every day after school he went to his room and read from the

Jackson biography. He was mesmerized by Jackson's life. When he read about the accidental shooting of Jackson by some of his own soldiers, he ran downstairs with tears in his eyes and told his parents, "Stonewall Jackson just got shot by his own men!" His parents realized how upset he was and did not laugh. That day "Stonewall" Jackson became Dr. Crewdson's favorite role model.

He read Douglas Southall Freeman's four volumes on Robert E. Lee while in boot camp and has continued to study the Civil War through the years. The first three parishes he served were either on or near battlefields. In 1962 he was active in the centennial anniversary of the Battle of Port Republic which was held at his first parish, Grace Church, which had been built as a memorial to the soldiers of both sides who lost their lives there.

In 1998, after serving parishes in Virginia, South Carolina, and North Carolina, Dr. Crewdson retired to Lexington, Virginia, where he resides with his wife, Lois, an award-winning artist and poet. In 2008 he became part-time chaplain to the Episcopal students of Washington and Lee University and the Virginia Military Institute for R. E. Lee Memorial Episcopal Church, and often supplies in small churches in the nearby four-county area.

Dr. Crewdson is also an avid hiker and backpacker, having completed the Appalachian Trail two and two-thirds times over the years. His trail name is "Backwards Bob," as he usually walks downhill backwards because of his knees and back. Hiking has been a cherished family hobby: His wife, Lois, has walked most of the Appalachian Trail and each of his sons has walked 500 miles as they were growing up. Dr. Crewdson now hikes with some of his grandchildren who have grown up with the hobby.

The Reverend Doctor Robert H. Crewdson

WITHDRAWN

APR - - 2010

4986210R0

Made in the USA
Lexington, KY
22 March 2010